THE QUILTER'S HOME

Spring

LOIS KRUSHINA FLETCHER

Martingale®
& COMPANY

CREDITS

President ✄ Nancy J. Martin
CEO ✄ Daniel J. Martin
Publisher ✄ Jane Hamada
Editorial Director ✄ Mary V. Green
Managing Editor ✄ Tina Cook
Technical Editor ✄ Laurie Baker
Copy Editor ✄ Mary Martin
Design Director ✄ Stan Green
Illustrator ✄ Laurel Strand
Cover and Text Designer ✄ Regina Girard
Photographer ✄ Brent Kane

That Patchwork Place® is an imprint of Martingale & Company®.

The Quilter's Home: Spring
© 2005 by Lois Krushina Fletcher

Martingale & Company
20205 144th Avenue NE
Woodinville, WA 98072-8478 USA
www.martingale-pub.com

Printed in China
10 09 08 07 06 05   8 7 6 5 4 3 2 1

MISSION STATEMENT

Dedicated to providing quality products and service to inspire creativity.

**Library of Congress
Cataloging-in-Publication Data**

Fletcher, Lois Krushina.
   The quilter's home : spring / Lois Krushina Fletcher.
      p. cm.
   ISBN 1-56477-592-5
   1. Patchwork—Patterns. 2. Quilting—Patterns.
3. Spring in art. I. Title.
   TT835.F57623 2005
   746.46'041—dc22

                              2004014848

DEDICATION

*In memory of my dear friend Judy Clark, whose
enthusiasm for living touched many lives.*

ACKNOWLEDGMENTS

I would like to begin by thanking my husband, Judge, for his undying support. He provides me the opportunity to fulfill my need to create, and for that I am extremely grateful. He is truly a blessing.

Once again my thanks go out to all of my friends who helped me test the patterns and instructions in this book: Cheri Ebens, Kathy Tilsy, Georgeanne Pinson, Sherry Moore, Ginger Helsten, Michelle Hale, and Kathy Alaniz. I also want to take this time to say a special thank-you to Kathy Tilsy, who was always just a phone call away when I needed her. Her input, suggestions, and help with last-minute finishing were priceless. Thanks also to Elizabeth Rushwam of Elizabeth's Creative Quilting for doing such a beautiful job of quilting the "Spring" Wall Hanging.

I would like to thank RJR Fabrics for its generosity in providing numerous fabrics used throughout this book. The border fabric from its Hint of Spring line was without a doubt the perfect fabric to depict the beauty of the season.

A big thank-you goes to Dean and Linda Moran of Marble-T Designs for providing the gorgeous hand-marbled fabrics used in the Crocus and Butterfly blocks. Their workmanship is exquisite, and their patience in getting me just the right colors was greatly appreciated.

Thanks also go to Starr Designs, Inc. of Etna, California, for supplying the hand-dyed fabrics used in the "Spring" and "April Showers" wall hangings.

Thanks to Ackfeld Manufacturing for supplying the ideal hangers for the "Spring Symphony" banners on page 65.

Contents

Introduction

I have always been excited by the prospect of a coming spring. Maybe it's the gardener in me, but after the lingering dreariness of winter, witnessing the earth's rebirth fills me with wonder. The succession of colors as leaves emerge and flowers begin to bloom is nothing less than spectacular. All around, the world seems fresh and clean, and colors seem exceptionally vivid and bright. Mother Nature paints glorious landscapes using her infinite palette, combining colors that even the most daring quilter would quite possibly never think of using. The result is always breath-taking.

I have tried to capture some of the glory of spring in this book. If you are familiar with the first two books in my Quilter's Home series, you may notice that many of the blocks in this book are the same dimensions. This was no accident. With just a little imagination, you can substitute many of the blocks from one book into the projects from the other. This increases your decorating options even more!

All of the projects in this book use either fusible-web appliqué, paper piecing, or a combination of the two in the construction process. The instructions for these techniques are presented in "Basic Techniques" on pages 7–12, so be sure to read through that section before embarking on any of the projects, even if you are already familiar with the processes.

When you're ready to complete your projects, turn to "Project Finishing" on pages 13–16. There you will find helpful advice for marking, layering, quilting, and binding your projects.

Basic Techniques

In this section, I describe techniques for making the blocks required for the projects in this book. Every quilter has her (or his) own way of doing things, so even if you are already accomplished at fusible-web appliqué and paper piecing, please take the time to read this section so you will be familiar with how I have presented the patterns and instructions.

TESTING FOR ACCURACY

The object when machine piecing is to sew with a scant ¼" seam allowance. The reason for this is that the bulk of the seams, especially when pressed to one side, takes up some of the fabric with its loft. If the seam measured exactly ¼", the finished piece would be too small. Even a slight difference in the size of the seam allowance can have a big impact on the final results. That is why the following test for accuracy is so important.

When testing your sewing machine for accuracy, start by using a ¼" foot if your machine has one. Although ¼" feet are made with quilters and machine piecing in mind, they do not necessarily give you the perfect scant ¼" seam allowance you need. If you discover that yours does not, try using other feet and/or needle positions, or try aligning the edge of the fabric at a slightly different position under the foot. I personally use my all-purpose foot with the needle position one click to the right, because I find it gives me greater accuracy than my ¼" foot. Experiment until you find the best presser foot, needle position, and/or guide, to give you the most accurate possible seam allowance. By taking the time to do this now, you will save more time

(and possible aggravation) later on by having pieces that fit together perfectly the first time.

To test your stitching for accuracy, do the following:

1. Cut 3 strips of fabric, each 1½" x 3".

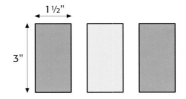

2. Sew the strips together along the long edges using a scant ¼" seam allowance. Press the seams to one side and measure the piece. Its width should now measure exactly 3½", and the center strip should measure exactly 1" across. If it does not, adjust your presser foot or needle position and repeat the test.

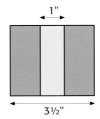

FUSIBLE-WEB APPLIQUÉ

One of the greatest developments in the world of quilting has to be the invention of paper-backed fusible web. It has opened up a whole new world to quilters who might never have tried the art of machine appliqué otherwise. I am one of them. In the beginning, only one type of fusible web was available, but with competition and demand came improvements. Now there are many different types to choose from, but for the projects in this book, select a lightweight web that you can sew through. (Do not attempt to use any fusible web that is separating from the paper! It is a waste of time and effort.)

When using fusible webs, prewash your fabrics. Fabrics are coated with sizing, which could potentially keep the adhesive from sticking properly. For that same reason, do not use fabric softeners of any kind, even dryer sheets, when prewashing and drying your fabrics.

One of the most important things to remember about fusible-web appliqué is that the appliqué design must be the reverse image of the finished design. All of the appliqué patterns in this book have already been reversed. If you are using hand appliqué methods, you will need to make mirror-image appliqué patterns and add turn-under allowances.

To make the appliqués for the projects in this book:

1. Follow the project instructions to trace the indicated appliqué patterns onto the paper side of the fusible web, leaving a small amount of space between each shape. Most of the appliqués are shown as they will be arranged on the background piece, which means some shapes will be overlapping others. To distinguish each individual appliqué, the outline of each pattern is shown in a different color than the shape(s) next to it. To trace the individual appliqués, follow the same color line, whether it is a solid line or a series of long dashed lines. The long dashed lines simply indicate where shapes overlap. You will refer to the lines when assembling the appliqué units, so make sure to trace them onto the appliqué shape. Any short dashed lines indicate detail stitching; you do not need to trace them onto the fusible web. Be sure to mark the pattern letter on each piece, because you will assemble the appliqué shapes in alphabetical order.

2. Cut out the traced shapes leaving a ⅛" margin. On large pieces, such as the bee skep, rabbit, and bonnet patterns, cut away the inner portion of the fusible-web shape to eliminate bulk and/or the background fabric showing through. Gently fold the fusible-web piece in half and make a small snip in the middle of the fold. Insert the tip of the scissors through the hole and cut ¼" to ⅜" from the inner edges.

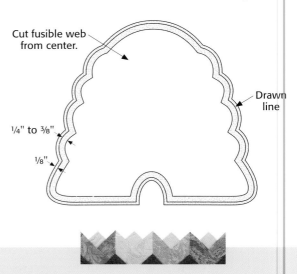

Cut fusible web from center.

Drawn line

¼" to ⅜"

⅛"

If you have a printed background that you do not want to show through the appliqué fabric (for example, the background behind the white fabric in the rabbit's body), you can cut away the background fabric after the appliqué has been stitched down if you have removed the center of the fusible-web shape as instructed in step 2 above. To do this, pull the background and appliqué fabrics away from each other and carefully make a small snip in the background fabric with a pair of scissors. Insert the tip of the scissors through the hole and trim the background fabric up to the edges where it was fused.

3. Follow the manufacturer's instructions to fuse the appliqué shapes to the wrong side of the appropriate fabrics.

4. Cut out the appliqué shapes on the drawn lines. Gently peel away the paper backing from the fabric.

If you have difficulty getting the paper to peel away from the fabric edge, lightly score the paper with the point of a pin. The paper will tear along the scored line, and you can begin the peeling process at that point. Be careful not to fray the edges of an appliqué piece by trying to force unwilling paper to separate from the fabric. The ragged edges that may result are more difficult to stitch down and might not adhere properly to the background fabric.

Your appliqué shapes are now ready to be fused to the background fabric. Do not fuse each individual shape onto the background fabric. Instead, make an appliqué unit. By making an appliqué unit, you can use the placement diagram and an appliqué pressing sheet to fuse all of the appliqués together first. Then you can position the fused unit onto the background fabric. You will eliminate guesswork when positioning the appliqués and achieve greater accuracy when centering the design on the background fabric.

To make an appliqué unit:

1. Make a placement diagram for the project. To do this, make a mirror-image photocopy of the appliqué patterns as they appear on the indicated page(s). If this option is not available on your photocopier, then photocopy or trace the appliqué patterns onto tracing or typing paper exactly as they appear on the indicated page(s). Turn the paper over and trace the image through to the blank side. A light source, such as a light box or window, makes this easier. Use the traced-through image as the placement diagram.

2. Put the placement diagram on the ironing surface. Lay the appliqué pressing sheet over the placement diagram and pin them both to the ironing-board cover with straight pins. This will prevent the layout from shifting while you are arranging the shapes.

3. Working in alphabetical order, place the appliqué shapes on the pressing sheet directly over the corresponding area on the placement diagram. The long dashed lines on the placement diagram indicate where the pieces overlap. Fuse the pieces together as they are layered on top of each other.

4. After all the pieces have been fused together, let the appliqué unit cool. Remove the unit from the pressing sheet. The fused shapes should easily peel away from the pressing sheet as one unit. If you notice some of the glue remaining on the appliqué pressing sheet as you peel off the fused unit, simply iron the unit back down and let it cool a little longer before removing.

5. Position the appliqué unit on the background fabric as indicated in the project instructions and fuse into place.

6. Refer to the appliqué patterns to mark any stitching detail lines, designated by short dashed lines, on the right side of the appliqués.

The edges of the individual appliqué shapes are now ready to be stitched down. The stitching not only secures the appliqués to the fabric, but it also prevents the appliqué edges from fraying when the project is washed or handled.

There are several ways to secure the edges. The first way is to use a satin stitch, which is a closely spaced zigzag stitch. The raw edge of the appliqué piece is aligned down the center of the stitches so that it is fully encased. For this method I prefer to use a 30-weight 100%-cotton thread in the needle in a color that matches the appliqué fabric, and white 60-weight 100%-cotton thread in the bobbin. Loosen the upper tension just a bit so that the top thread pulls slightly to the underside of the appliqué. I recommend using tear-away stabilizer underneath the background fabric when satin stitching. It will eliminate puckers and help the edges of the appliqué lie smooth and flat. Carefully remove the stabilizer after the stitching is complete. While mastery of satin stitching does take some practice, especially if a lot of curves or corners are involved, the result can be very attractive and worth the time it takes to master it.

A similar method of securing fusible appliqué edges is simply to use a small zigzag stitch. For this method, I use clear monofilament in the needle and white 60-weight 100%-cotton thread in the bobbin. Once again, align the appliqué raw edges down the center of the stitches.

Last, there is the machine blanket stitch, or buttonhole stitch, which is becoming more widely available as a built-in stitch option on sewing machines. When done in a thread color that contrasts with the appliqué, this stitch gives the project an antique or country look. I use black 100%-cotton quilting thread in the needle and black 100%-cotton all-purpose thread in the bobbin for this method. One important difference when using a machine blanket stitch, as opposed to a zigzag or satin stitch, is that the appliqué raw edge is placed adjacent to the straight-stitch portion of the blanket stitch, not centered in the middle as with the other two methods.

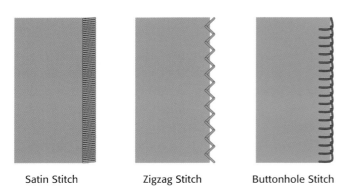

Satin Stitch   Zigzag Stitch   Buttonhole Stitch

PAPER PIECING

With paper piecing, as with any technique, there are several ways to achieve the same result. Whatever way works best for you is the "right" way. The methods described here are those that I have found, through trial and error, work best for me.

In paper piecing, the foundation pattern is the reverse image of the completed block because the block is sewn from the back of the printed pattern. The following is a brief description of how paper piecing is done. If this technique is new to you, I suggest following detailed guidelines, such as those contained in Carol Doak's *Show Me How to Paper Piece* (Martingale & Company, 1997). There you will find step-by-step instructions, as well as clear photographs, for learning the technique.

Paper Piecing Single Units

1. Photocopy or trace the foundation pattern onto a lightweight paper that provides a clear image, is easy to tear away, and does not transfer ink to the fabric.

2. The foundation sections are numbered and will be sewn in order numerically. Cut a piece of fabric big enough to cover section 1. Place the wrong side of the fabric piece against the unprinted side of the foundation pattern, making sure that it covers section 1 on all sides by at least ¼". Pin in place from the paper side.

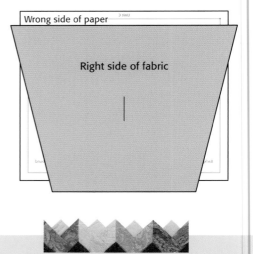

Wrong side of paper

Right side of fabric

Instead of pinning the first piece of fabric to the paper foundation, try using a restickable or repositionable glue stick. These are available in many office supply stores or scrapbooking departments of craft stores. Swipe the glue stick over the back of section 1 (and only section 1) on the foundation paper. Position your fabric piece over the section and finger-press it into place. The glue will hold the fabric in place while you position piece 2 over it. Just be sure you don't accidentally use a permanent glue stick!

3. Turn the fabric side up. With right sides together, place a piece of fabric big enough to cover section 2 over the section 1 piece, making sure that the fabric edge extends past the line between sections 1 and 2 by at least ¼".

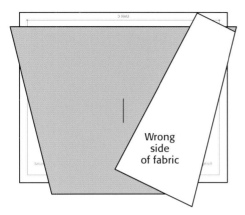

Wrong side of fabric

4. Reduce the stitch length on your machine to 18 to 20 stitches per inch. Holding the fabric for section 2 in place, turn the foundation unit to the paper side and stitch along the line between sections 1 and 2, beginning and ending a few stitches beyond both ends of the line. Remove the pins.

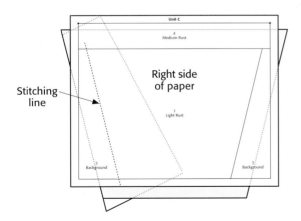

Stitching line

Right side of paper

5. With the paper side up, fold back the paper along the seam line and trim the seam allowance to ¼". Turn the foundation unit to the fabric side and press the fabric open so that it covers section 2.

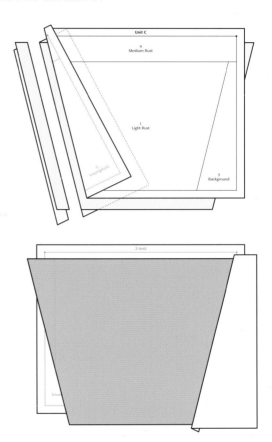

6. Repeat this process until all of the sections have been covered with fabric. Turn the completed unit to the paper side and trim the block along the outer dashed line. To prevent any bias edges from stretching when handled, do not remove

the paper until the block has been set in the quilt, unless specified in the project instructions.

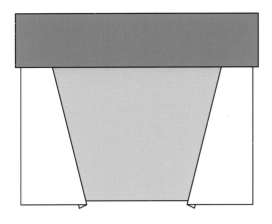

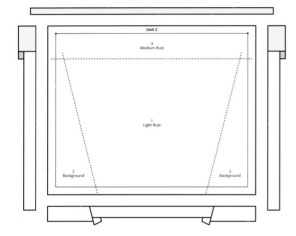

Joining Multiple Units

There are several paper-piecing foundations used throughout this book that require one or more separate paper-pieced units to be stitched together to complete the block (for example, the Watering Can, Robin, and Bearded Iris blocks). Here's how to do it:

1. Paper piece each unit as described in the preceding section, "Paper Piecing Single Units." Be sure to mark the alignment dots and the unit letter on each pattern when tracing the foundations.

2. From the paper side, push a straight pin through the first alignment dot of unit A. Push the pin all the way through the fabric until the head of the pin is flush with the paper.

3. Now, push the pin through the fabric side of unit B so that it emerges through the corresponding alignment dot on the paper side of the unit. Push unit B up the pin to meet unit A. Make sure the pin head is still flush with the paper in unit A.

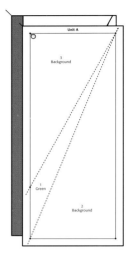

4. While holding units A and B firmly, pin them together right next to the alignment pin with a second pin, being careful not to shift the fabric layers in the process. Remove the alignment pin.

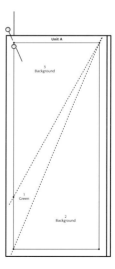

5. Repeat steps 3 and 4 with the remaining alignment dots. Stitch the 2 units together along the outer solid line of unit A. Remove the paper from the seam allowances only. Press the seam in the direction indicated in the project instructions.

Project Finishing

*W*hether you have made a wall hanging, a pillow sham, or a table topper, this section will help you with general finishing instructions to complete your project. Specific instructions are included with each project. All of the projects in this book were machine quilted, but you may, of course, hand quilt if you prefer.

MARKING THE TOP FOR QUILTING

I like to mark all my quilting lines, except those that will be stitched in the ditch or stipple quilted. If you choose to mark the project top, you must do it after the completed top is pressed and before the top is layered. Pressing the top after it is marked could permanently set the marks.

Many suitable marking tools are available. My favorites are a fine-point mechanical pencil for light-color fabrics and, more recently, the Clover white marking pen for dark-color fabrics. I tried this new pen and now it is virtually the only tool I use for marking darker fabrics. It makes a very fine white line upon drying, much finer than the silver pencil that I used to use, and the lines are erasable with either water or heat. I occasionally use a water-erasable blue marker for light-color fabrics, but if you choose to use one, be prepared to dampen the marks several times to remove them, because they tend to reappear as the fabric dries. I have never had this problem when using heat to erase the white marker, but do not use heat to erase the blue marker! It may set the lines. Whichever marking tool you choose, be sure to test it on a scrap of fabric first to make sure that the lines are visible as well as removable.

ASSEMBLING THE LAYERS

The next step is to layer the top with backing and batting.

1. Cut the backing and batting at least 2" larger than the project top on all sides. In some cases, you will need to piece the backing fabric to make a large enough piece. Be sure to trim off the selvages if these edges will be seamed. Press the seam open.

2. Place the backing wrong side up on a clean, flat surface, such as a table or floor. Secure it on all sides with masking tape, or use 1" binder clips to fasten the backing to the table edges. The backing should be taut, but be careful not to stretch it out of shape or the finished project could pucker. Place the batting on top of the backing and smooth it in place. I find that the long edge of an acrylic ruler works better than my hand for smoothing out the batting. Lastly, place the quilt top on the batting, right side up. Center it over the batting and smooth out any wrinkles.

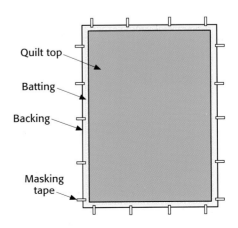

3. The backing, batting, and quilt top now need to be basted together to keep them from shifting as the project is handled and to keep the backing and batting smooth and pucker-free. The three most common basting tools are thread, safety pins, and tacks. On smaller projects, you may wish to try one of the new spray-basting glues, which make quick work of the basting process. These sprays provide a temporary bond and allow the top to be repositioned if needed. Simply follow the instructions on the can. If you are machine quilting, I recommend safety pins, because you can remove them as you quilt. I prefer to use 1" safety pins. Place the pins about 4" apart in all directions. It is not necessary to place them in an exact grid; it is better to place them where they will not interfere with the quilting lines. It is easier to insert all of the pins first, and then go back and close them all.

QUILTING

For straight-line quilting and some in-the-ditch quilting, a walking foot is necessary for optimal results. Both the top and bottom fabrics feed under this type of presser foot at the same rate, which helps to keep the layers from shifting during quilting. For any other quilting, I recommend free-motion quilting, which requires that you drop the feed dogs and use a darning foot. Once you establish the correct motor speed and the correct rate at which to move the fabric to produce a consistent stitch, free-motion quilting is just a matter of practice. The best tip I can give you is to relax your shoulders and try not to tense up. Let your movements flow naturally and your quilting lines will flow with them.

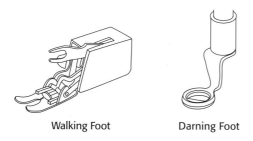

Walking Foot   Darning Foot

It is easier to see what you're quilting, and it places less strain on your shoulders, if the bed of your machine is angled forward slightly. An inexpensive way to achieve this is to purchase two rubber wedge-shaped doorstoppers. Insert them under the back edge of your machine, on opposite sides. Try this and see what a difference it makes!

When it is necessary to begin or end a stitching line in the middle of a quilt, reduce the stitch length and take several tiny stitches. The threads will be secure and can be cut flush with the top and backing of the project. Do not make several stitches in the same hole, because the threads will form a knot on the back of the quilt.

BINDING THE EDGES

I prefer a French double-fold binding, which is made using strips of fabric that are cut on grain. I do not trim the edges of my batting and backing until the binding is sewn to the project top. This gives more control over the exact amount of batting left in the seam allowance, which results in a binding that is full all the way to the fold.

To bind the project edges:

1. Cut the binding strips as indicated in the project cutting instructions.

2. Place two binding strips at right angles to each other, right sides together. Draw a diagonal line on the top strip where the edges of the 2 strips intersect. Stitch along the drawn line. Trim the seam allowance to ¼" and press the seam open. Repeat with any remaining strips to make one long strip.

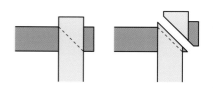

Joining Straight-Cut Binding Strips

3. Cut one end of the binding strip at a 45° angle. Press the binding strip in half lengthwise, wrong sides together and raw edges matching.

Fold line

4. Beginning with the angled end of the binding strip, align the raw edge of the strip with the raw edge of the project top, centering the beginning of the strip on the project top. On larger projects, such as the "Spring" wall hanging, begin stitching 8" to 10" from the angled end, using a walking foot and a ¼" seam allowance. Smaller projects, such as the "Robin" wall hanging, will require less "tail" at the end. Stop ¼" from the corner of the project top; backstitch and clip the threads.

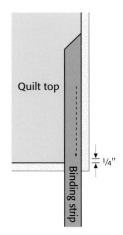

Quilt top

Binding strip

¼"

5. Turn the project so that the next seam to be sewn is in front of you. Fold the binding up to create a 45°-angle fold.

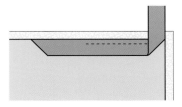

6. Fold the binding down, the fold even with the top edge of the project and the raw edge aligned with the side of the project. Beginning slightly off the edge of the binding, stitch the binding to the project, stopping ¼" from the next corner. Backstitch and clip the threads. Continue the folding and stitching process for the remaining corners.

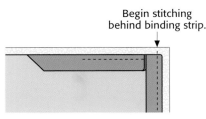

Begin stitching behind binding strip.

7. When you return to the edge where you began, end the stitching approximately 12" to 15" away from the beginning stitches; backstitch and clip the threads. (On smaller items, the distance will naturally be smaller.)

8. Lay the quilt flat and place the beginning tail on top of the ending tail. Place a mark on the ending tail where it meets the beginning tail. Place another mark ½" to the right of the first mark.

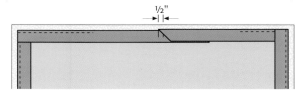

½"

9. Open out the ending tail strip and align the 45° line of a small Bias Square® ruler with the top edge of the opened binding strip. Place the ruler point on the mark that was ½" from the beginning tail mark. Cut the ending tail strip along the edge of the ruler as shown. The ends of both binding strips should now be cut at a 45° angle and overlap ½".

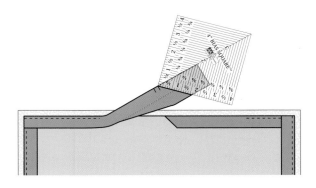

10. Join the binding ends, right sides together, using a ¼" seam allowance. (It is helpful to fold the quilt out of the way when doing this.) Press the seam open and refold the binding. Finish stitching the binding to the quilt top.

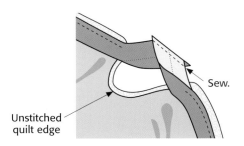

Sew.

Unstitched quilt edge

11. Trim the backing and batting ⅜" from the binding *stitching line*.

12. Gently press the right side of the binding away from the project top, using just the tip of the iron. Fold the binding to the back of the project over the raw edges, covering the machine stitching. Insert a straight pin directly into the ditch of the binding seam on the front of the project. Push the pin through all layers and bring it back up in the ditch about ½" away, being sure that the folded edge of the binding has been caught in the pin on the back of the project. Continue pinning the binding in place around the entire edge of the project. Miter the binding corners on the back of the project by forming a tuck when pinning them in place.

Quilt top

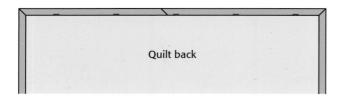

Quilt back

13. On the right side of the quilt, stitch in the ditch to secure the binding, removing the pins as the needle of the sewing machine approaches them.

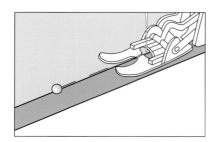

Remove pins as they approach the needle.

ATTACHING A HANGING SLEEVE

Not all of the projects require a hanging sleeve, but for those that do, here are the steps:

1. Cut a piece of fabric 8" wide (less if it is a small project) and 1" shorter than the width of the project. Press the short ends under ¼" twice. Stitch close to the first folded edge.

2. Press the strip in half lengthwise, wrong sides and raw edges together. Unfold the strip and refold the long edges to meet the center crease; press the folded edges.

Center crease →

3. Open up the strip and fold it in half lengthwise, wrong sides together. Stitch the long edges together to form a tube, backstitching at the beginning and end of the seam. Center the seam in the middle of the tube and press the seam allowance open, using the tip of the iron. Be careful not to press another crease in the edges while pressing the seam open, because the previous creases will be used as stitching lines.

4. Center the fabric sleeve on the back of the project just under the binding on the top edge, with the seam allowance facing the project. Be sure the seam side of the sleeve lies flat against the backing fabric. The top side of the sleeve will have a small amount of slack in it to allow room for a hanging rod and will not lie flat. Slip-stitch the sleeve in place along the creased edges of the sleeve, and on the bottom layer at each end. Be sure not to stitch through to the right side of the quilt.

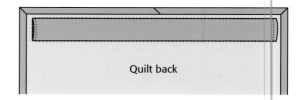

Quilt back

"Spring" Wall Hanging

This section contains instructions for making the blocks that compose the "Spring" wall hanging and for assembling the wall hanging itself. The blocks are arranged in order of complexity, so beginners may find it helpful to start with block 1 and progress through block 11.

You will notice that most of the appliquéd blocks are trimmed after the appliqué is applied. This is because appliqué, regardless of which application method you use, tends to draw up the background fabric to some extent. The more pieces you appliqué to a block, the more the background tends to "shrink." Be sure to trim an even amount from all four sides so the design remains centered.

Fabric requirements are listed for each individual block. If you plan to make the wall hanging using the same background fabric throughout, purchase a total of 2½ yards. Because some of the blocks call for cut pieces and some are paper pieced, cut all the straight-cut segments from one end of the fabric and all of the paper-piecing segments from the other end to help conserve fabric.

BLOCK 1: SPRING

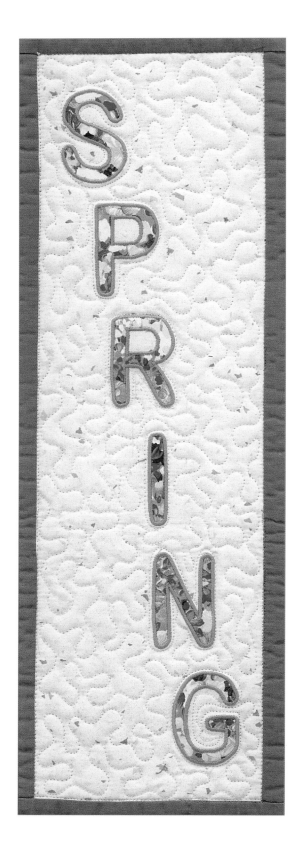

Finished block size: 6" x 18"

MATERIALS

Yardage is based on 42"-wide fabric.

- ⅛ yard of solid green for outer border
- 6" x 18" rectangle of neutral print for background
- 6" x 6" square of floral print for appliqué letters
- 6" x 6" square of paper-backed fusible web

CUTTING

All measurements include ¼"-wide seam allowances.

From the solid green, cut:

2 strips, 1" x 42". Crosscut to make:

- 2 strips, 1" x 17½", for side borders
- 2 strips, 1" x 6½", for top and bottom borders

ASSEMBLING THE BLOCK

1. Referring to "Fusible-Web Appliqué" on pages 7–10, trace the patterns on page 20 onto the paper side of the fusible web. Trace 1 *each* of A–F. Cut around the shapes. Fuse each shape to the wrong side of the floral print. Cut out the appliqués on the drawn lines and remove the paper backing. Use the patterns on page 20 to make a placement diagram, aligning the dashed lines to make the complete diagram. Using the placement diagram, center the appliqués on the right side of the neutral-print 6" x 18" rectangle, positioning shape A 1¼" from the top edge and 1" from the left edge of the background rectangle. Fuse in place.

2. Machine stitch around the edges of each appliqué shape, using either a buttonhole stitch, satin stitch, or zigzag stitch.

3. Trim the block to 5½" x 17½", keeping the design centered.

4. Stitch the 1" x 17½" green strips to the side edges of the quilt block. Press the seams toward the border strips. Stitch the 1" x 6½" green strips to the top and bottom edges of the quilt block. Press the seams toward the border strips.

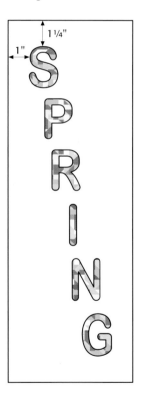

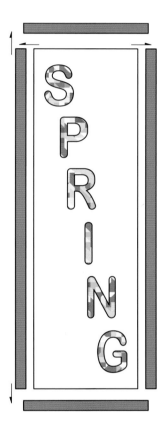

Block 1: Spring
Appliqué Patterns

Align with dashed line below.

Align with dashed line above.

BLOCK 2: POSIES

Finished block size: 6" x 6"

MATERIALS

Materials listed are enough to make 4 blocks.

- 4 squares, 7" x 7", of neutral print for background
- 7" x 7" square of pink for flowers
- 7" x 7" square of yellow for flowers
- 7" x 7" square of lavender for flowers
- 4" x 6" rectangle of green for leaves
- 12" x 12" square of paper-backed fusible web
- Appliqué pressing sheet
- 12 yellow ¾"-diameter buttons for flower centers

ASSEMBLING THE BLOCKS

1. Referring to "Fusible-Web Appliqué" on pages 7–10, trace the appliqué patterns on page 22 onto the paper side of the fusible web. Trace 4 *each* of A–D. Cut around the shapes. Fuse 4 of each appliqué shape to the wrong side of the appropriate fabrics. Cut out the appliqués on the drawn lines and remove the paper backing. Use the patterns on page 22 to make a placement diagram. Using an appliqué pressing sheet and the placement diagram, fuse the appliqué shapes together.

2. Center an appliqué unit on the right side of each of the background squares. Fuse in place.

3. Machine stitch around the edges of each appliqué shape, using either a buttonhole stitch, satin stitch, or zigzag stitch.

4. Trim the blocks to 6½" x 6½", keeping the designs centered.

5. After the project is completed, stitch a button to the center of each flower where indicated.

Block 2: Posies
Appliqué Patterns

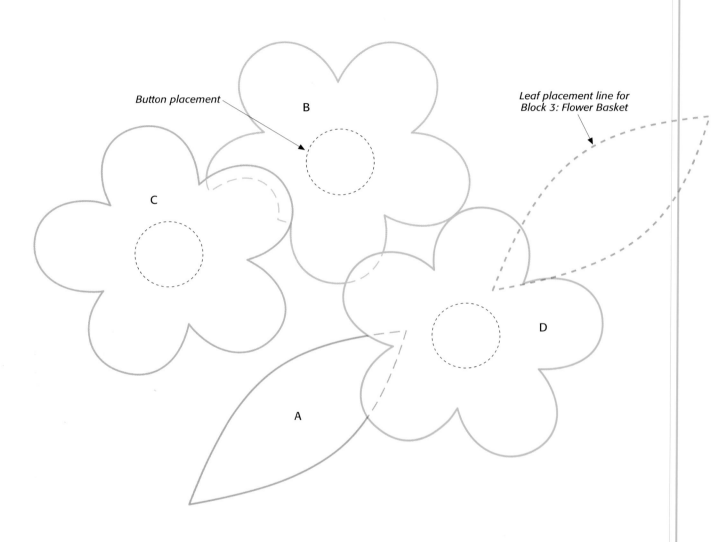

Button placement

B

C

Leaf placement line for
Block 3: Flower Basket

D

A

BLOCK 3: FLOWER BASKET

Finished block size: 9" x 12"

MATERIALS

Yardage is based on 42"-wide fabric.

- ¼ yard of neutral print for background
- ¼ yard of brown basket-weave print for basket
- 3" x 3" square of pink for flower
- 3" x 3" square of yellow for flower
- 3" x 3" square of lavender for flower
- 2" x 3" rectangle of green for leaf
- Foundation paper
- 6" x 6" square of paper-backed fusible web
- Appliqué pressing sheet
- 3 yellow ¾"-diameter buttons for flower centers
- One ⅜"-diameter ladybug button (optional)

ASSEMBLING THE BLOCK

1. Referring to "Paper Piecing" on pages 10–12, photocopy or trace the foundation patterns on pages 24 and 25 onto separate pieces of foundation paper. Matching the corresponding lines on section I and section II, tape the pieces of paper together to make the complete foundation pattern. Paper piece the foundation, referring to the pattern for the appropriate fabric to use in each section. Turn the block to the paper side and trim to 9½" x 12½" along the dashed lines. Carefully remove the paper foundation.

    Note: *Because appliqué pieces will be added to this block, the paper must be removed before the block is set into the quilt. Handle the block carefully so as not to distort any bias edges.*

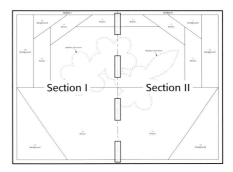

2. Referring to "Fusible-Web Appliqué" on pages 7–10, trace the appliqué patterns for Block 2: Posies (page 22) onto the paper side of the fusible web. Trace 1 *each* of A–D. Cut around the shapes. Fuse each appliqué shape onto the wrong side of the appropriate fabric. Cut out the appliqués on the drawn lines and remove the paper backing. Use the patterns on page 22 to make a placement diagram. (Note that the leaf has a different placement line than on the Posies block.) Using an appliqué pressing sheet and the placement diagram, fuse the appliqué shapes together.

3. Using the placement lines on the foundation pattern and the photo above as a guide, fuse the appliqué unit in place.

4. Machine stitch around the edges of each appliqué shape, using either a buttonhole stitch, satin stitch, or zigzag stitch.

5. After the project is completed, stitch a button to the center of each flower where indicated. If desired, stitch the ladybug button on the leaf.

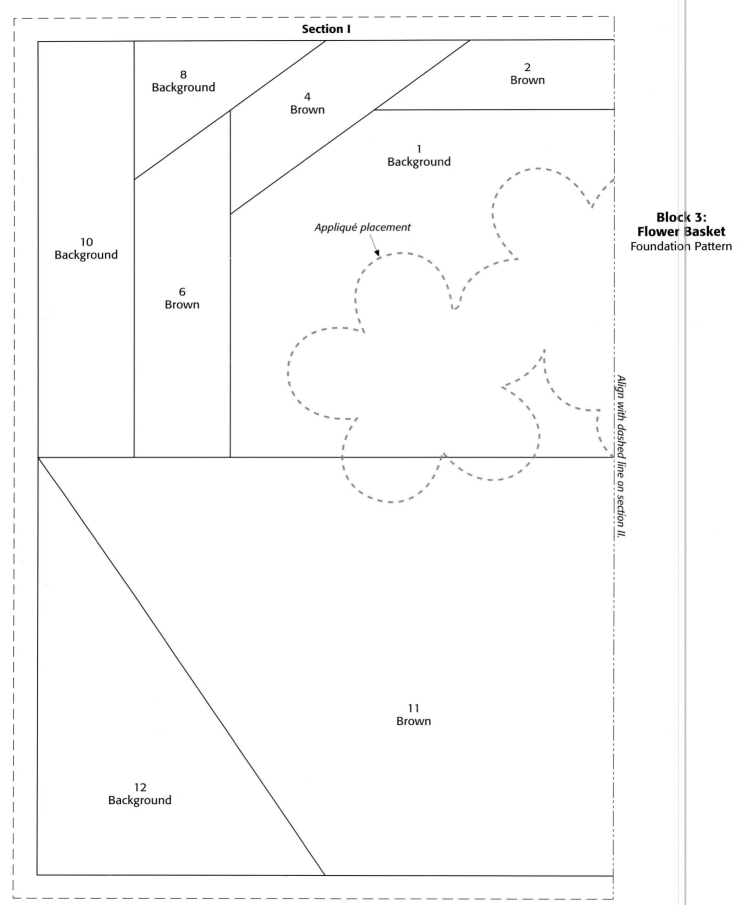

Section I

8
Background

2
Brown

4
Brown

1
Background

Appliqué placement

10
Background

6
Brown

Block 3:
Flower Basket
Foundation Pattern

Align with dashed line on section II.

11
Brown

12
Background

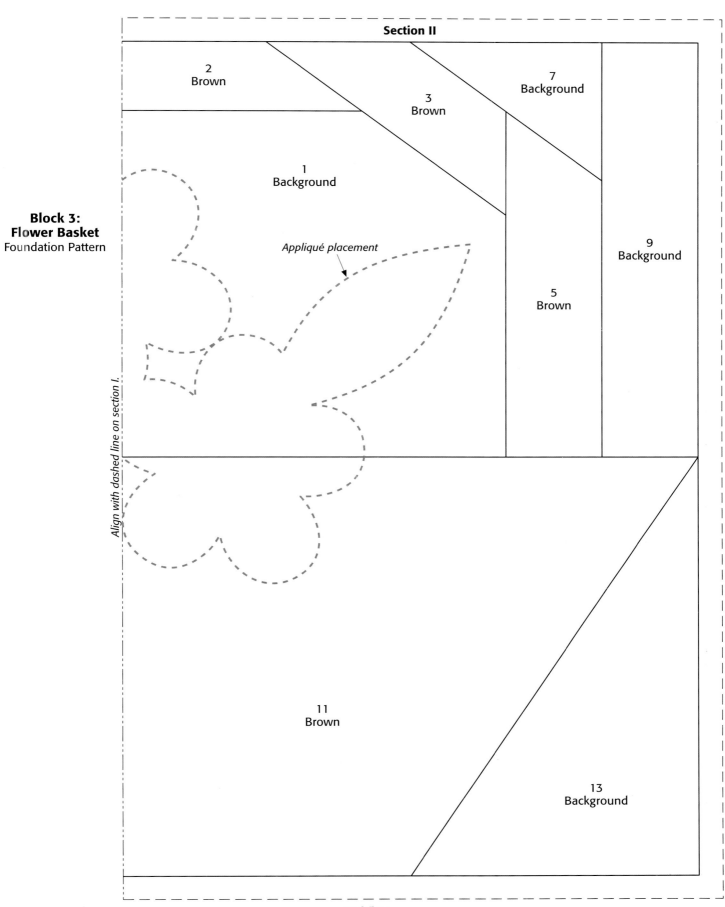

Section II

2
Brown

3
Brown

7
Background

1
Background

Appliqué placement

9
Background

5
Brown

**Block 3:
Flower Basket**
Foundation Pattern

Align with dashed line on section I.

11
Brown

13
Background

BLOCK 4: TULIP

Finished block size: 6" x 6"

MATERIALS

Yardage is based on 42"-wide fabric.
Materials listed are enough to make 5 blocks.

- ¼ yard of neutral print for background
- ¼ yard of medium green for leaves
- Scraps of medium pink, medium lavender, and medium yellow for flower petals
- Scraps of dark pink, dark lavender, and dark yellow for flower centers
- Foundation paper

ASSEMBLING THE BLOCKS

1. Referring to "Paper Piecing" on pages 10–12, use the pattern on page 27 to photocopy or trace 5 Tulip foundations onto foundation paper.
2. Paper piece the foundations, referring to the pattern for the appropriate fabric to use in each section.
3. Turn the blocks to the paper side and trim to 6½" x 6½" along the dashed lines. Do not remove the paper foundation until the blocks are set into the project. This will eliminate any stretching that can occur when the bias edges are handled.

Block 4: Tulip
Foundation Pattern

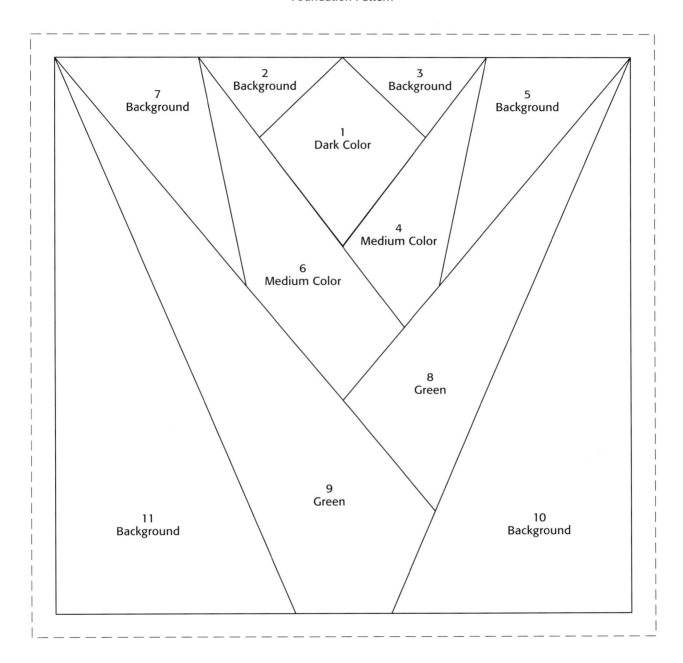

BLOCK 5: BONNET

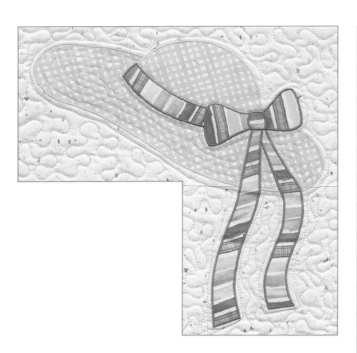

Finished block size: 12" x 12"
(including Block 1)

MATERIALS

- 6½" x 12½" rectangle of neutral print for background
- 6½" x 6½" square of neutral print for background
- 6" x 12" rectangle of yellow plaid for bonnet
- 7" x 9" rectangle of multicolored stripe for hatband and bow
- 12" x 12" square of paper-backed fusible web
- Appliqué pressing sheet

ASSEMBLING THE BLOCK

Because this block is built in conjunction with one Block 1: Spring block (page 18) and two Block 4: Tulip blocks (page 26), you will need to complete them first.

1. Referring to "Fusible-Web Appliqué" on pages 7–10, trace the appliqué patterns on pages 29 and 30 onto the paper side of the fusible web. Trace 1 *each* of A–G. Cut around the shapes, removing the fusible web inside shape A, if desired.

2. Fuse each appliqué shape to the wrong side of the appropriate fabric. When placing shapes B–G on the striped fabric, align the arrows on the appliqué patterns parallel with the fabric stripes. Cut out the appliqués on the drawn lines and remove the paper backing.

3. Use the patterns on pages 29 and 30 to make 2 placement diagrams. Using an appliqué pressing sheet and the placement diagram, fuse the unit I (bow) shapes together first. When cool, remove from the pressing sheet and fuse the unit II (bonnet) shapes together. Before removing unit II from the appliqué pressing sheet, position unit I in place and fuse it onto unit II.

4. Sew the Tulip blocks together vertically. Sew the 6½" x 6½" background square to the top Tulip block, as shown on the following page. Sew this unit to the right side of Block 1. Sew

the 6½" x 12½" background rectangle to the top of this unit as shown. Press all seams as indicated.

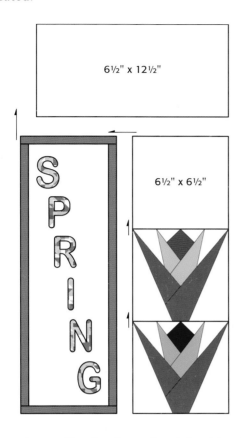

5. Center the appliqué unit on the right side of the background pieces, referring to the photo on page 17 for placement. Fuse in place.

6. Machine stitch around the edges of each appliqué shape, using either a buttonhole stitch, satin stitch, or zigzag stitch.

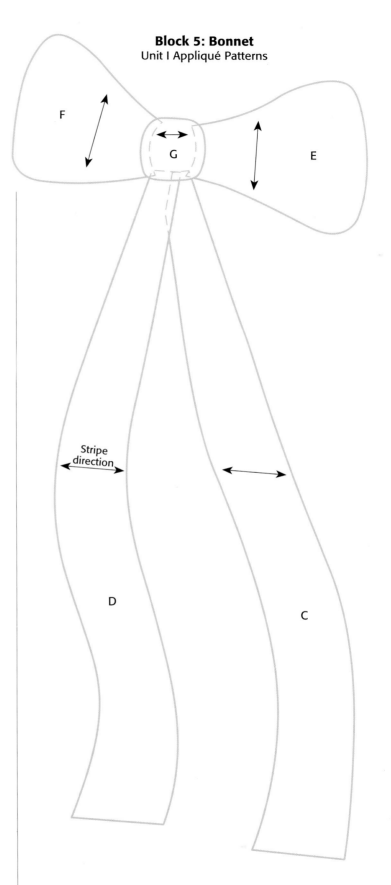

Block 5: Bonnet
Unit I Appliqué Patterns

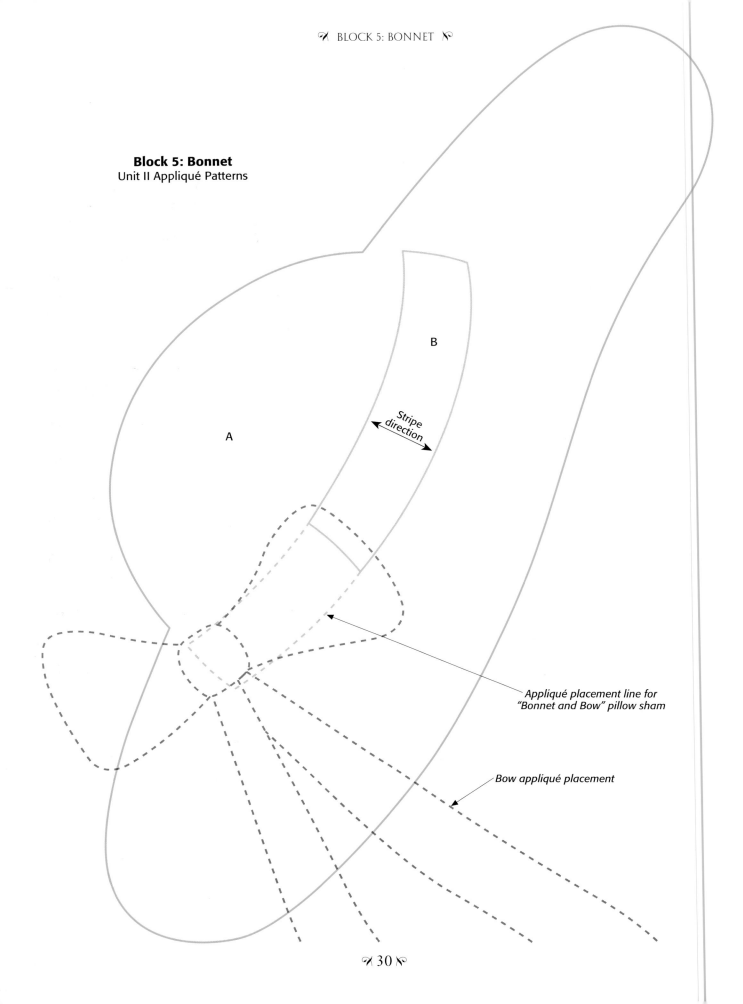

Block 5: Bonnet
Unit II Appliqué Patterns

A

B

Stripe
direction

Appliqué placement line for
"Bonnet and Bow" pillow sham

Bow appliqué placement

BLOCK 6: BUTTERFLY

Finished block size: 9" x 9"

MATERIALS

- 10" x 10" square of neutral print for background
- 8" x 8" square of solid black for butterfly background
- 8" x 8" square of yellow-orange for butterfly wings*
- 12" x 12" square of paper-backed fusible web
- Black thread for antenna detail lines
- Hand embroidery needle (optional)

    * *Slightly more fabric may be needed if you fussy cut from a marbled fabric as shown.*

ASSEMBLING THE BLOCK

1. Referring to "Fusible-Web Appliqué" on pages 7–10, trace the appliqué patterns on page 32 onto the paper side of the fusible web. Trace 1 *each* of A–I. Cut around the shapes. Fuse each appliqué shape to the wrong side of the appropriate fabric. Cut out the appliqués on the drawn lines and remove the paper backing. Be sure to cut out the areas within the dotted lines on piece A as indicated.

2. Because the butterfly is a symmetrical design, there is no need to reverse it to make the placement diagram. Simply trace the appliqué pattern as drawn. Using an appliqué pressing sheet and the placement diagram, fuse the butterfly background in place. Align shapes B–I over each corresponding cutout on piece A and fuse in place.

3. Referring to the photo as a guide, position the butterfly appliqué on the background square at an angle as shown; fuse in place.

4. Machine stitch around the edges of each appliqué shape, using either a buttonhole stitch, satin stitch, or zigzag stitch. Stitch over the detail lines on the butterfly body, if desired. Hand or machine embroider over the antenna detail lines using black thread.

5. Trim the block to 9½" x 9½", keeping the design centered.

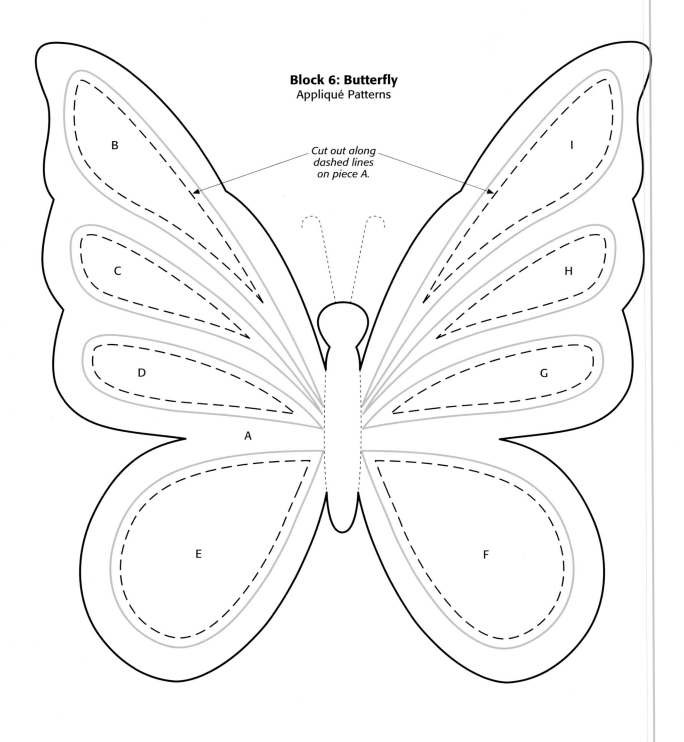

Block 6: Butterfly
Appliqué Patterns

*Cut out along
dashed lines
on piece A.*

BLOCK 7: BEARDED IRIS

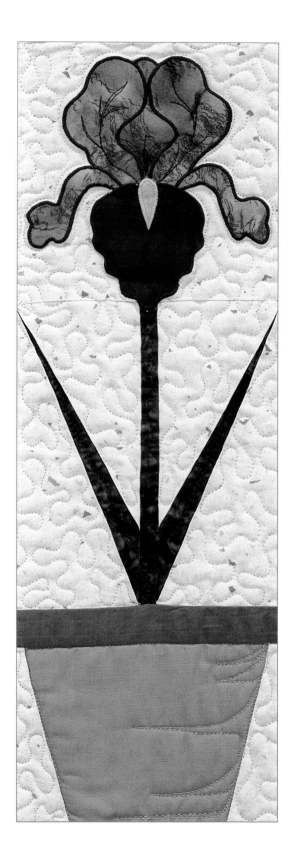

MATERIALS

Yardage is based on 42"-wide fabric.

- ¼ yard of neutral print for background
- 6" x 7" rectangle of light rust for flowerpot
- 6" x 7" rectangle of light purple for upper flower
- 4" x 4" square of dark purple for lower flower
- 2" x 8" rectangle of medium rust for flowerpot rim
- Scrap of medium green for stem and leaves
- Scrap of yellow for iris "beard"
- Foundation paper
- 7" x 7" square of paper-backed fusible web
- Appliqué pressing sheet

CUTTING

Measurement includes ¼"-wide seam allowance.

From the neutral print, cut:

1 square, 6½" x 6½"

ASSEMBLING THE BLOCK

1. Referring to "Paper Piecing" on pages 10–12, photocopy or trace the foundation patterns on pages 35 and 36 onto foundation paper. Paper piece each unit, referring to the pattern for the appropriate fabric to use in each section of each unit.

2. After all the pieces have been added, trim only the edges of each unit that will be joined to another unit. Stitch the units together in the order shown on the following page. When all

the units have been joined, remove the paper from the seam allowances only. Press the seams as shown. Turn the block to the paper side and trim to 6½" x 12½". Carefully remove the paper foundation from the stem unit.

Note: Because appliquéd pieces will be added to the stem unit of the block, the paper must be removed before the block is set into the quilt. Handle the block carefully so as not to distort any bias edges.

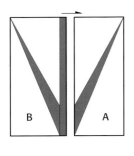

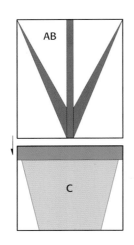

3. With right sides together, sew the 6½" x 6½" background square to the top of the stem. Press the seam toward the background square.

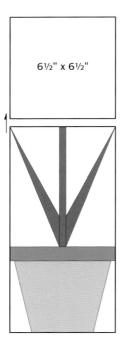

4. Referring to "Fusible-Web Appliqué" on pages 7–10, trace the appliqué patterns on page 37 onto the paper side of the fusible web. Trace 1 *each* of A–C. Cut around the shapes. Fuse each appliqué shape to the wrong side of the appropriate fabric. Cut out the appliqués on the drawn lines and remove the paper backing. Because the iris is a symmetrical design, there is no need to reverse it to make the placement diagram. Simply trace the appliqué pattern as drawn. Using an appliqué pressing sheet and the placement diagram, fuse the appliqué shapes together.

5. Center the appliqué unit on the right side of the background square, having the bottom of the iris just covering the top of the iris stem as noted on the appliqué pattern. Fuse in place.

6. Mark the stitching detail lines on the upper iris.

7. Machine stitch around the edges of each appliqué shape and over the detail lines, using either a buttonhole stitch, satin stitch, or zigzag stitch.

Block 7: Bearded Iris
Foundation Patterns

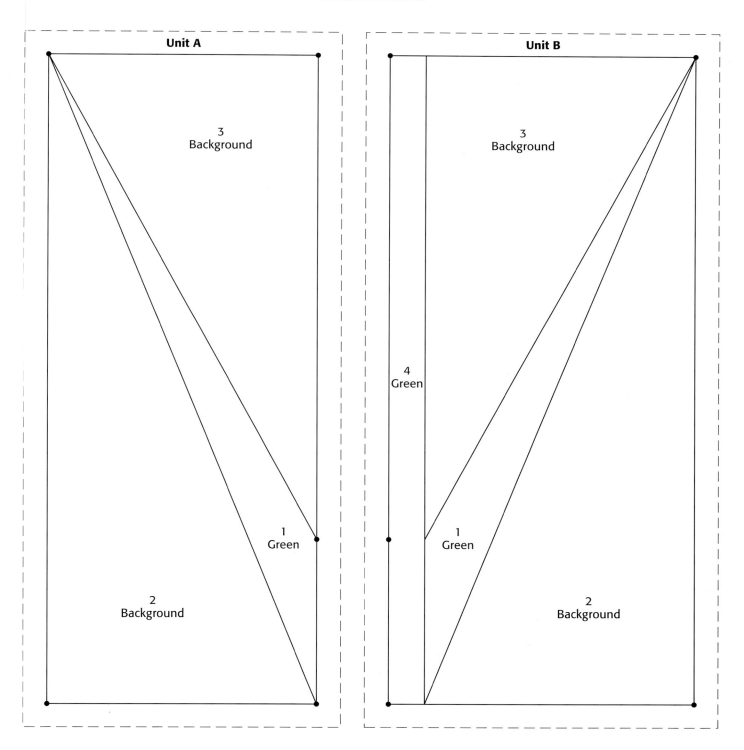

Block 7: Bearded Iris
Foundation Pattern

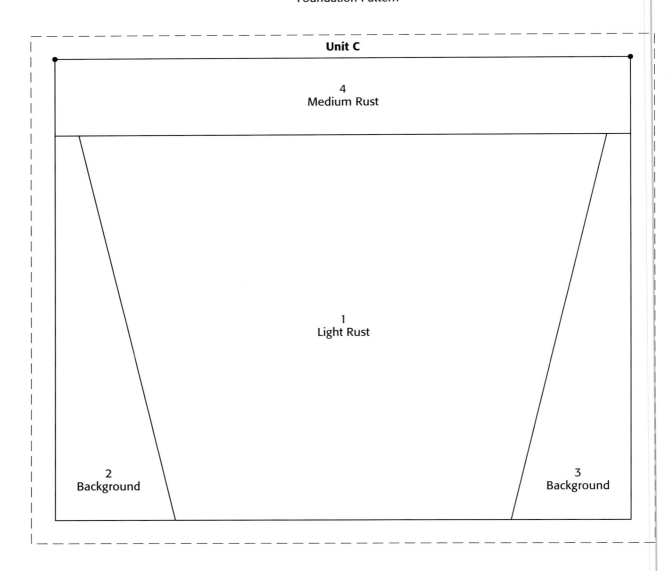

Unit C

4
Medium Rust

1
Light Rust

2
Background

3
Background

Block 7: Bearded Iris
Appliqué Patterns

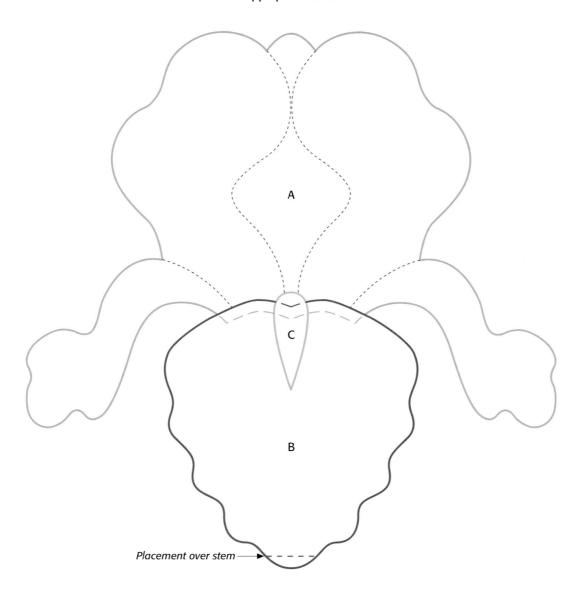

A

C

B

Placement over stem →

BLOCK 8: WATERING CAN

Finished block size: 12" x 12"

MATERIALS

Yardage is based on 42"-wide fabric.

- ½ yard or 1 fat quarter of gray for watering can
- ¼ yard of neutral print for background
- Foundation paper

CUTTING

All measurements include ¼"-wide seam allowances.

From the neutral print, cut:

1 strip, 1½" x 42". Crosscut to make:

- 2 strips, 1½" x 12½", for top and bottom of watering can

1 rectangle, 3" x 4⅛"

1 rectangle, 3" x 4⅝"

ASSEMBLING THE BLOCK

1. Referring to "Paper Piecing" on pages 10–12, photocopy or trace the foundation patterns on pages 39–41 onto foundation paper. Paper piece each unit, referring to the pattern for the appropriate fabric to use in each section of each unit.

2. After all of the pieces have been added, trim only the edges of each unit that will be joined to another unit. Stitch units A, B, C, and D together in the order shown. Remove the paper from the seam allowances only and press the seams in the directions indicated. Turn the block to the paper side and trim unit ABCD to 8" x 12½" along the outside dashed lines.

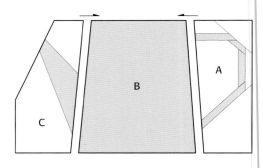

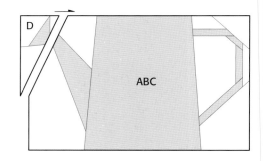

3. Trim unit E to 3" x 4¾" along the outside dotted lines. Stitch the 3" x 4⅝" neutral print rectangle to the left side of unit E. Stitch the 3" x 4⅛" neutral print rectangle to the right side of unit E. Stitch this unit E strip to the top of unit ABCD. Press the seam toward unit E. Stitch a 1½" x 12½" neutral strip to the top and bottom of the watering can as shown. Verify that the block measures 12½" x 12½" and trim if necessary.

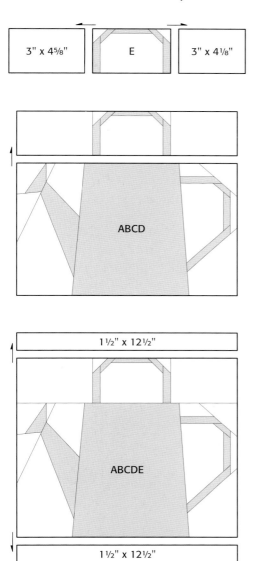

Block 8: Watering Can
Foundation Pattern

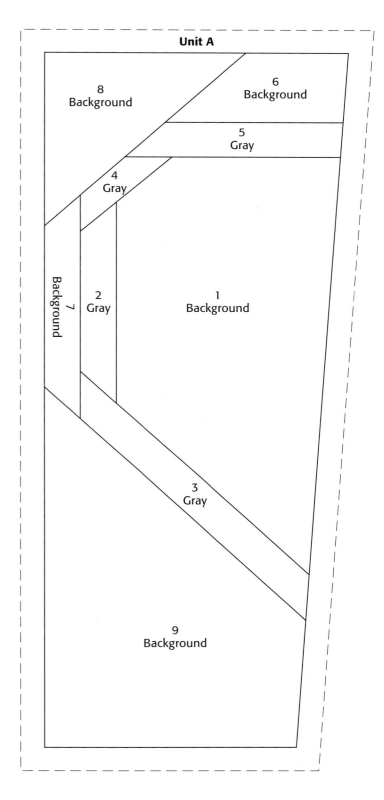

Block 8: Watering Can
Foundation Pattern

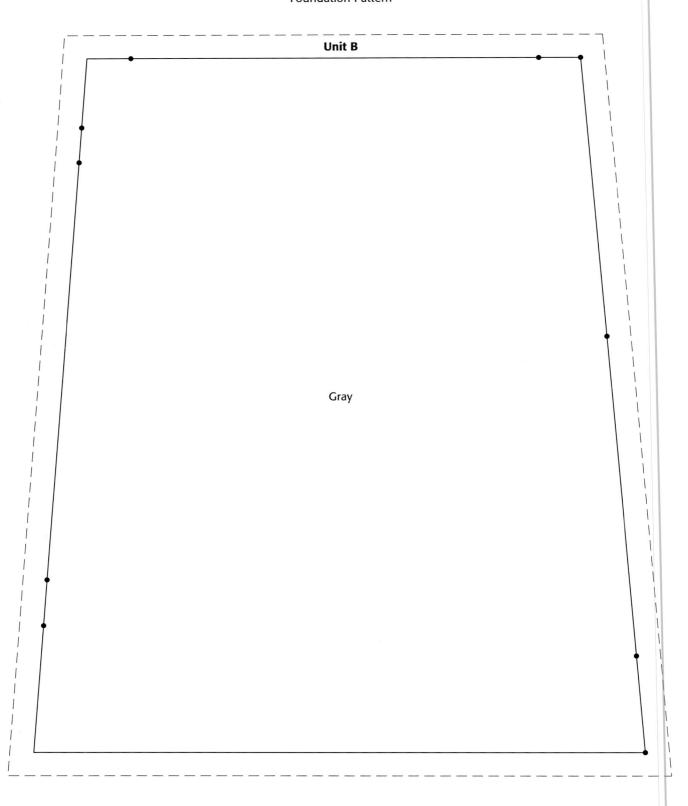

Unit B

Gray

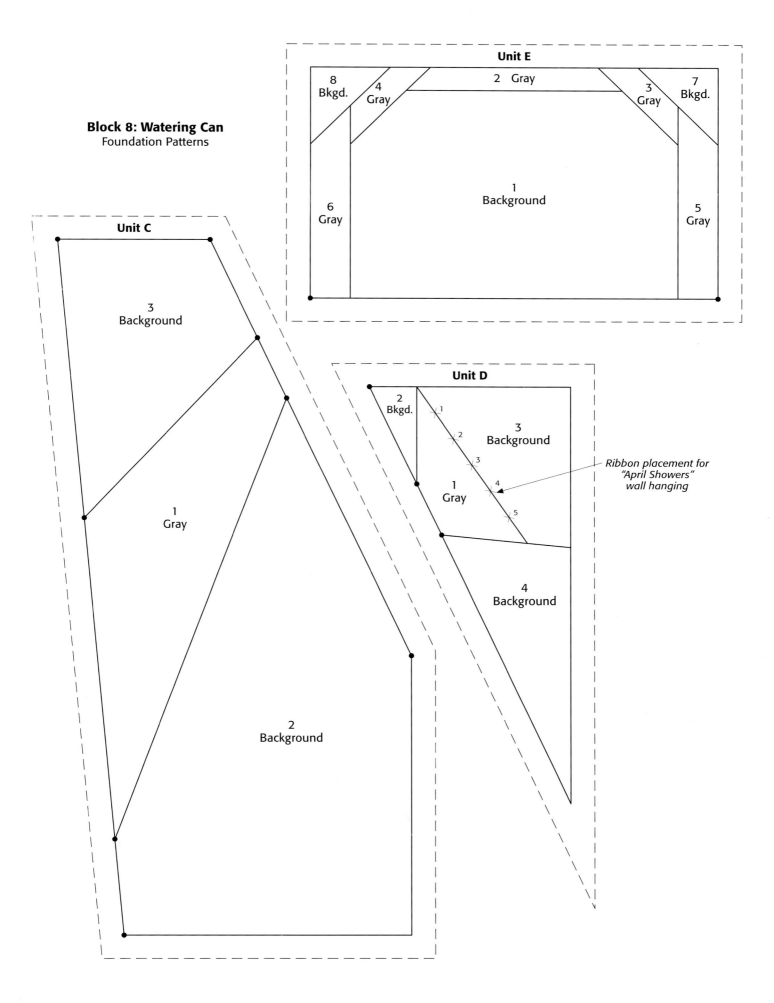

Block 8: Watering Can
Foundation Patterns

Unit E

8 Bkgd.

4 Gray

2 Gray

3 Gray

7 Bkgd.

6 Gray

1 Background

5 Gray

Unit C

3 Background

1 Gray

2 Background

Unit D

2 Bkgd.

3 Background

1 Gray

4 Background

1
2
3
4
5

Ribbon placement for "April Showers" wall hanging

BLOCK 9: RABBIT

Finished block size: 9" x 12"

MATERIALS

- 6¾" x 13" rectangle of neutral print for background top
- 3¾" x 13" rectangle of green grass print for background bottom
- 6" x 10" rectangle of dark brown for rabbit body and head
- 7" x 7" square of white for rabbit body, foot, and tail
- 2" x 2" square of pink for rabbit nose and inside ear
- 1" x 1" square of black for rabbit eye
- 10" x 12" square of paper-backed fusible web
- Appliqué pressing sheet

ASSEMBLING THE BLOCK

1. With right sides together, sew the neutral and green background rectangles together along the 13" edges. If the green fabric is directional, be sure to have the rectangle oriented in the right direction. Press the seam open.

2. Referring to "Fusible-Web Appliqué" on pages 7–10, trace the appliqué patterns on page 43 onto the paper side of the fusible web. Trace 1 *each* of A–H. Cut around the shapes, removing fusible web inside the larger shapes, if desired. Fuse each appliqué shape to the wrong side of the appropriate fabric. Cut out the appliqués on the drawn lines and remove the paper backing. Use the pattern on page 43 to make a placement diagram. Using an appliqué pressing sheet and the placement diagram, fuse the appliqué shapes together.

3. Center the appliqué unit on the right side of the background rectangle. Fuse in place.

4. Mark the stitching detail lines on the rabbit's body and head.

5. Machine stitch around the edges of each appliqué shape, using either a buttonhole stitch, satin stitch, or zigzag stitch. Continue the stitching along the detail lines on the rabbit's body.

6. Trim the block to 9½" x 12½", keeping the design centered.

Block 9: Rabbit
Appliqué Patterns

BLOCK 10: BEE SKEP AND BEES

Finished block size: 12" x 12"

MATERIALS

- 13" x 13" square of neutral print for background
- 10" x 10" square of gold basket-weave print for bee skep
- 6" x 6" square of light gray for bee wings
- 6" x 6" square of black for bee bodies and bee skep entrance
- 2 strips, ¾" x 6", of yellow for bee stripes
- 6" x 8" rectangle of paper-backed fusible web
- Appliqué pressing sheet

CUTTING

All measurements include ¼"-wide seam allowances.

From the black square, cut:

1 strip, ¾" x 6", for bee bodies

2 strips, 1" x 6", for bee bodies

ASSEMBLING THE BLOCK

1. Referring to "Fusible-Web Appliqué" on pages 7–10, trace the appliqué patterns on pages 45 and 46 onto the paper side of the fusible web. Trace 1 *each* of A–C, 5 *each* of D and F, 2 of E, and 3 of E reversed. *Be sure to trace the detail lines on all of the E shapes.* Cut around the shapes, removing the fusible web inside shape B, if desired. Fuse shapes A–D and F to the wrong side of the appropriate fabrics. Cut out the appliqués on the drawn lines and remove the paper backing.

2. Use the patterns on page 46 to make a placement diagram for the bee skep. Using an appliqué pressing sheet and the placement diagram, fuse appliqué shapes A–C together.

3. Sew a ¾" x 6" yellow strip to each side of the ¾" x 6" black strip. Trim the seam allowances to ⅛" and press open. Sew a 1" x 6" black strip to the long side of each yellow strip. Trim the seam allowances to ⅛" and press open. This resulting pieced unit will now be used as the foundation fabric for shapes E and E reversed.

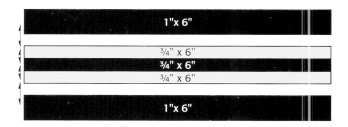

4. Fuse shapes E and E reversed to the wrong side of the pieced unit from step 3, aligning the detail lines over the seam lines. Cut out the appliqués on the drawn lines and remove the paper backing.

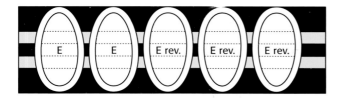

5. Because the patterns at right are reversed images, they can be used as placement diagrams for each other. Using an appliqué pressing sheet and the placement diagrams, fuse appliqué shapes D, E or E reversed, and F together, making two Bee 1 units and three Bee 2 units.

6. Place the bee skep appliqué unit on the right side of the background square, having the lower-left corner 1¼" from the left and bottom edges of the background square as shown. Fuse in place. Referring to the photo on page 44 as a guide, arrange the bees around the skep; fuse in place.

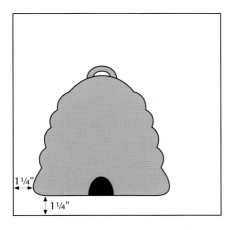

7. Machine stitch around the edges of each appliqué shape, using either a buttonhole stitch, satin stitch, or zigzag stitch.

Because the seam allowances in the bee bodies will prevent the appliqué units from fusing tightly to the background fabric, you may find it helpful to use a stiletto to hold the edge down in front of the sewing-machine needle while stitching.

8. Trim the block to 12½" x 12½", trimming evenly from each side.

Block 10: Bee Skep and Bees
Appliqué Patterns

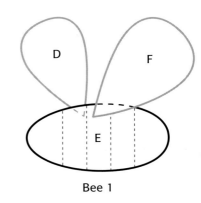

Bee 1

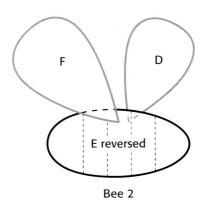

Bee 2

Block 10: Bee Skep and Bees
Appliqué Patterns

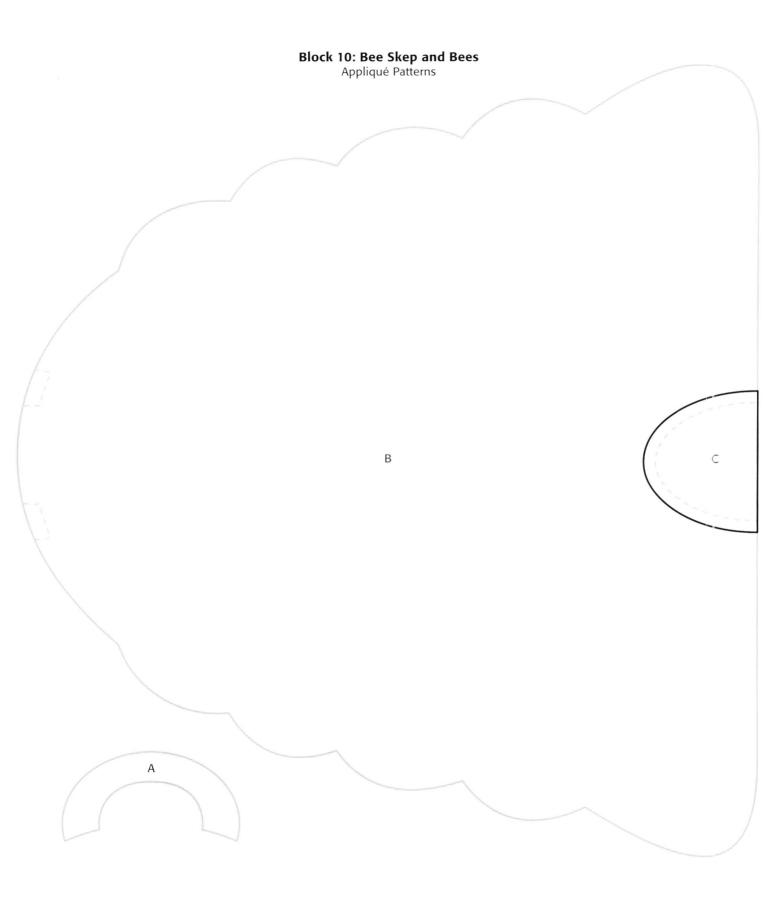

B

C

A

BLOCK 11: ROBIN

Finished block size: 9" x 12"

MATERIALS

Yardage is based on 42"-wide fabric.

- ¼ yard of neutral print for background
- Scrap of rust for robin breast
- Scrap of dark gray for robin wing and head
- Scrap of medium gray for robin back
- Scrap of dark gold for robin beak
- Scrap of brown for branches
- Scrap of medium blue for eggs
- Scrap of medium brown for nest
- Scrap of dark brown for inside nest
- Scrap of green for leaves
- Foundation paper
- 6" x 6" square of paper-backed fusible web
- Appliqué pressing sheet
- 1 black ⅛"-diameter button for robin eye

CUTTING

Measurement includes ¼"-wide seam allowance.

From the neutral print, cut:

1 rectangle, 3½" x 9½", for left side of robin block

ASSEMBLING THE BLOCK

1. Referring to "Paper Piecing" on pages 10–12, photocopy or trace the foundation patterns on pages 49 and 50 onto foundation paper. Paper piece each unit, referring to the pattern for the appropriate fabric to use in each section of each unit.

2. After all of the pieces have been added, trim only the edges of each unit that will be joined to another unit. Stitch units A–E together in the order shown. Remove the paper from the seam allowances only and press the seams in the directions indicated. Turn the block to the paper side and trim to 9½" x 9½" along the outside dashed lines. Carefully remove the paper foundation. Sew the 3½" x 9½" rectangle to the left side of the block.

   Note: *Because appliqué pieces will be added to this block, the paper must be removed before the block is set into the quilt. Handle the block carefully so as not to distort any bias edges.*

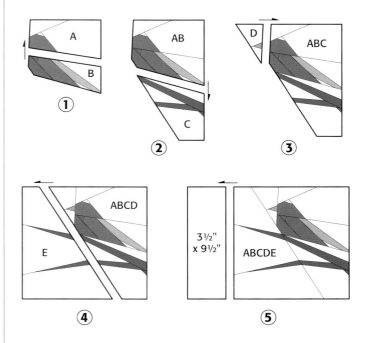

3. Referring to "Fusible-Web Appliqué" on pages 7–10, trace the appliqué patterns below onto the paper side of the fusible web. Trace 1 *each* of A–D and 3 of E. Cut around the shapes. Fuse each appliqué shape to the wrong side of the appropriate fabric. Cut out the appliqués on the drawn lines and remove the paper backing. Use the patterns below to make a placement diagram. Using an appliqué pressing sheet and the placement diagram, fuse appliqué shapes A–D together.

4. Using the placement line on the foundation pattern and the photo on page 47 as a guide, fuse the appliqué unit and leaves in place.

5. Machine stitch around the edges of each appliqué shape, using either a buttonhole stitch, satin stitch, or zigzag stitch.

6. After the project is completed, stitch the black button to the bird's head where indicated for the eye.

Block 11: Robin
Appliqué Patterns

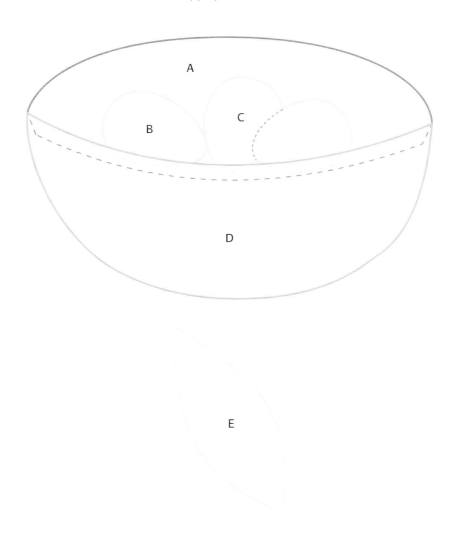

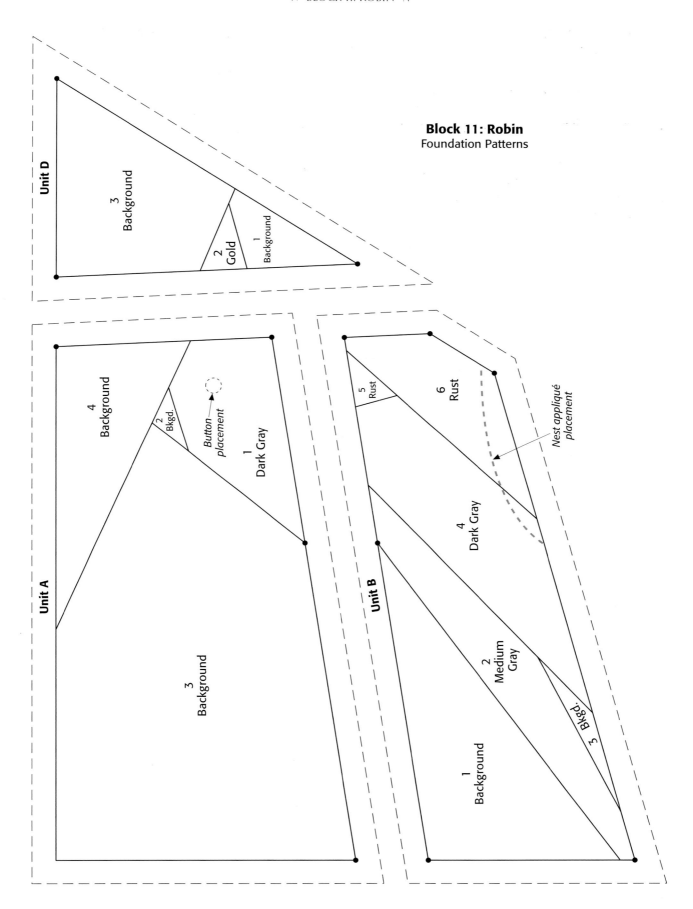

Block 11: Robin
Foundation Patterns

Unit D

3 Background

2 Gold

1 Background

Unit A

4 Background

2 Bkgd.

Button placement

1 Dark Gray

3 Background

Unit B

5 Rust

6 Rust

4 Dark Gray

Nest appliqué placement

2 Medium Gray

3 Bkgd.

1 Background

Block 11: Robin
Foundation Patterns

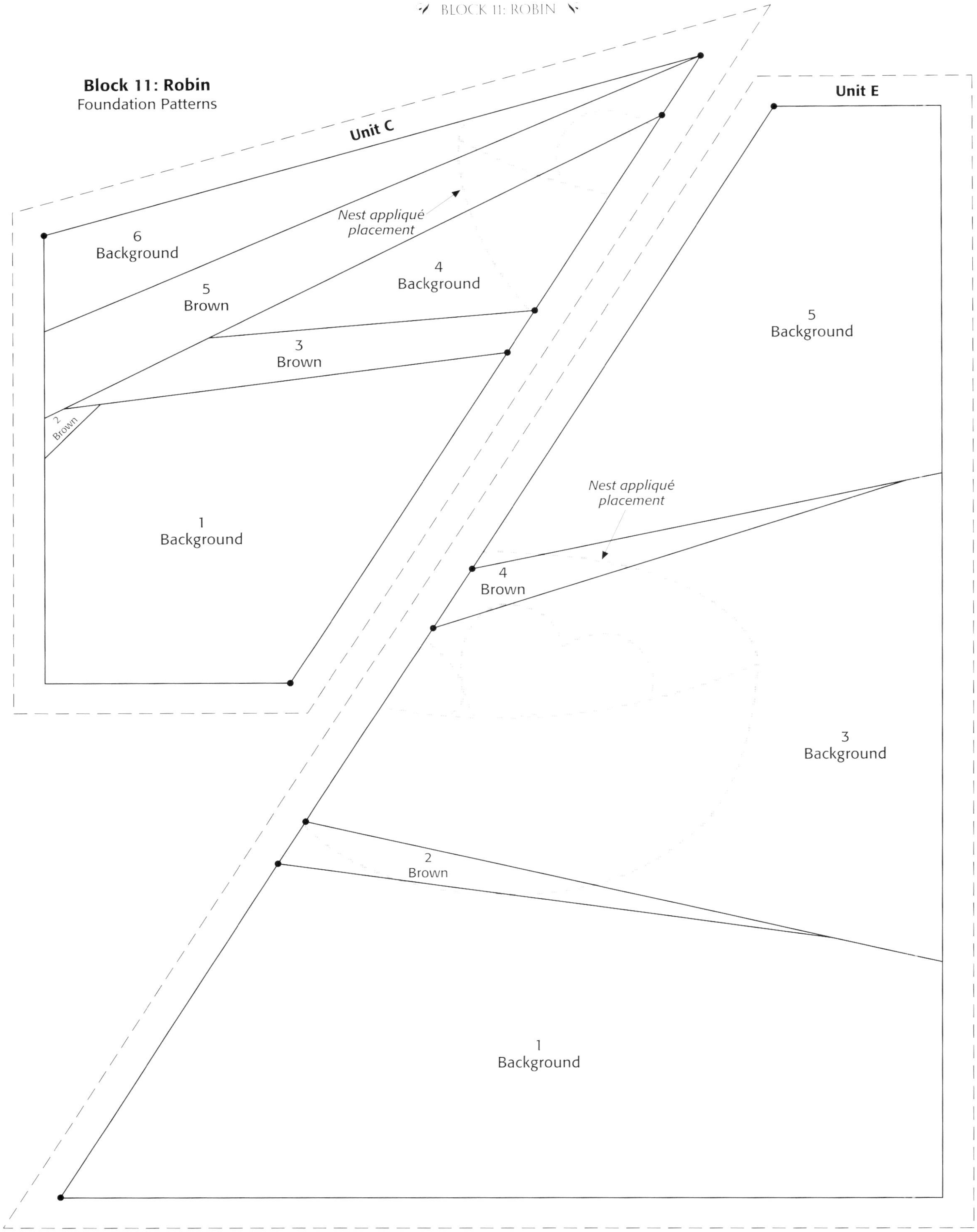

Unit C

Unit E

6
Background

5
Brown

4
Background

Nest appliqué placement

3
Brown

2
Brown

1
Background

5
Background

Nest appliqué placement

4
Brown

3
Background

2
Brown

1
Background

CROCUS BLOCKS

Finished block size: 3" x 3"

MATERIALS

Yardage is based on 42"-wide fabric.
Materials listed are enough to make 11 blocks.

- ¼ yard of neutral print for background
- ¼ yard of medium green for leaves
- ¼ yard each of light pink, light blue, lavender, and yellow marbled fabrics for flower petals
- Scraps of solid yellow for flower centers
- Foundation paper

ASSEMBLING THE BLOCKS

Referring to "Paper Piecing" on pages 10–12, photocopy or trace 11 foundation patterns below onto foundation paper. Paper piece the foundation units, referring to the pattern for the appropriate fabric to use in each section. Turn the blocks to the paper side and trim to 3½" x 3½" along the dashed lines. Do not remove the paper foundation until the blocks are set into the project. This will eliminate any stretching that might occur when the bias edges are handled.

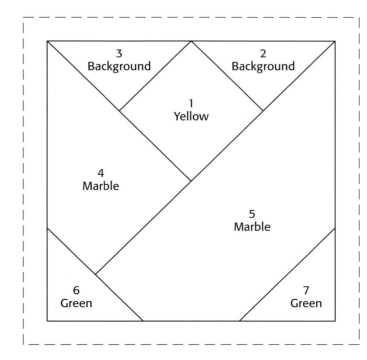

Crocus Block
Foundation Pattern

WALL-HANGING CONSTRUCTION

his colorful wall hanging captures the essence of the season. From the delicate first flowers to the return of butterflies to the nesting birds, each block in the quilt is a snapshot of spring.

Finished wall-hanging size: 51" x 51"

MATERIALS

Yardage is based on 42"-wide fabric. In addition to the following items, you will need the materials listed for blocks 1–11 on pages 18–50 and for the Crocus blocks on page 51. If you plan to make the wall hanging using the same background fabric throughout, purchase a total of 2½ yards.

- ¾ yard of green solid for inner borders and binding
- ¾ yard of neutral background fabric for outer border
- ¾ yard of floral print for outer border
- 3⅜ yards of fabric for backing
- Twin-size batting
- Heavy cardboard or template plastic

CUTTING

All measurements include ¼"-wide seam allowances.

From the green solid, cut:

4 strips, 1½" x 42", for inner border. Crosscut to make:

- 2 strips, 1½" x 36½", for inner side borders
- 2 strips, 1½" x 38½", for inner top and bottom borders
- 6 strips, 2½" x 42", for binding

From the neutral print, cut:

3 strips, 6¾" x 42", for outer-border triangles

From the floral print, cut:

2 strips, 6¾" x 42", for outer-border triangles

4 rectangles, 5½" x 7", for outer-border end triangles

From the backing, cut:

2 rectangles, 27½" x 54"

From the batting, cut:

1 square, 54" x 54"

ASSEMBLING THE WALL-HANGING TOP

1. Refer to the block instructions on pages 18–50 to make 1 each of blocks 1, 3, and 5–11. Make 4 of block 2 and 5 of block 4. Refer to page 51 to make 11 Crocus blocks. The materials listed for each block will make the required number.

2. Sew the Crocus blocks into strips as shown. Make 2 horizontal strips of 4 Crocus blocks and 1 vertical strip of 3 Crocus blocks.

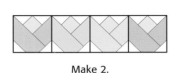

Make 2.

Make 1.

3. Arrange the blocks and Crocus strips into 3 vertical rows as shown. Stitch the blocks and the Crocus strips in each row in the order shown. Press the seam allowances in the direction shown. Stitch the rows together.

4. For the inner border, stitch the green 1½" x 36½" strips to the wall-hanging sides. Press the seams toward the strips. Stitch the green 1½" x 38½" strips to the top and bottom edges of the wall hanging. Press the seams toward the strips.

5. To make the outer-border triangles, trace the template pattern on page 56 onto heavy cardboard or template plastic and cut out on the drawn line. Stack the 3 neutral print strips on top of each other so that all of the edges are aligned. Working on a flat cutting surface, place the long edge of the template along the cut edge of the fabric strips. Cut the first set of 3 triangles. Rotate the template 180° and cut the next set of 3 triangles. Repeat this procedure to cut 16 neutral-print background triangles. Repeat the procedure with the floral 6¾" x 42" strips to cut 12 triangles.

Template

6. Place 2 floral 5½" x 7" rectangles *right sides together.* Cut in half diagonally from corner to corner. Repeat with the remaining rectangles to make 8 outside-border end triangles.

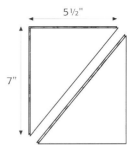

5½"

7"

7. Beginning and ending with a neutral-print outer-border triangle, alternately stitch 4 background triangles and 3 floral-print triangles together. Stitch an end triangle to each end of the strip. Make 4.

Make 4.

8. Sew an outer-border strip to the top and bottom edges of the quilt top, placing the floral-print fabric next to the inner border. Press the seams toward the inner border. Stitch 1 block 2 to each end of the remaining border strips as shown on the following page. Stitch the border strips to the sides of the quilt top. Press the seams toward the inner border.

FINISHING THE WALL HANGING

1. Refer to "Project Finishing" on pages 13–16 to layer, quilt, and bind the wall hanging.

2. Sew the buttons to the rabbit (block 9) for the eye, the posy centers (blocks 2 and 3), and the robin (block 11) for the eye, where indicated. If desired, sew a ladybug button to the leaf in block 3.

3. Refer to "Attaching a Hanging Sleeve" on page 16 to sew a hanging sleeve to the back of the quilt.

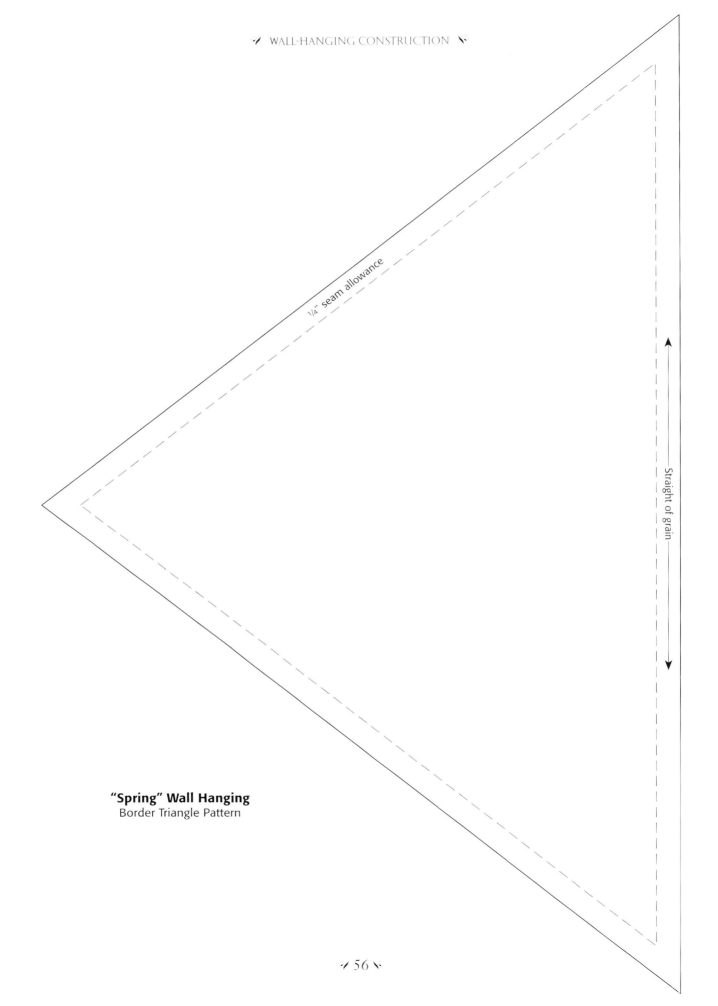

¼" seam allowance

Straight of grain

"Spring" Wall Hanging
Border Triangle Pattern

"Tea-Hive" Tea Cozy

This cozy little beehive—I mean, tea-hive—will keep your teapot warm while you relax and sip your tea. It fits over a standard four-cup teapot and coordinates with the "Busy Bee" Mug Rugs (page 62).

Finished cozy size: 9" x 12"

MATERIALS

Yardage is based on 42"-wide fabric.

- ¾ yard of honeycomb print for background and lining
- 10" x 10" square of gold basket-weave print for bee skep
- 3" x 6" rectangle of light gray for bee wings
- 3" x 5" rectangle of black for bee bodies and bee skep entrance
- 2 strips, ¾" x 3", of yellow for bee stripes
- 2 rectangles, 11" x 14", of muslin for backing
- 2 rectangles, 11" x 14", of batting
- 8" x 9" rectangle of paper-backed fusible web
- Appliqué pressing sheet
- 1 wooden curtain ring with a ¾" inside diameter
- Black quilting thread for detail stitching
- Hand quilting needle (optional)

CUTTING

All measurements include ¼"-wide seam allowances.

From the black rectangle, cut:

1 strip, ¾" x 3", for bee bodies

2 strips, 1" x 3", for bee bodies

From the honeycomb print, cut:

2 strips, 11" x 42". Crosscut to make:

- 4 rectangles, 11" x 14", for background and lining
- 1 rectangle, 1" x 4", for tab

ASSEMBLING THE TEA COZY

1. Referring to "Block 10: Bee Skep and Bees" on page 44, make one bee skep appliqué unit, using the appliqué patterns on page 46. Referring to

The rear side of the "Tea-Hive" tea cozy is buzzing with excitement.

steps 3–5, make the pieced unit for the bee bodies, substituting the 3"-long black and yellow strips for the 6"-long black and yellow strips. Make 2 Bee 1 appliqué units using the patterns on page 45. Center the bee skep appliqué unit on one of the 11" x 14" honeycomb rectangles, placing the bottom of the skep 1" from the bottom edge of the block. Fuse in place. Fuse one of the bee appliqué units to the bee skep as shown. This will be the front of the tea cozy.

2. Place the remaining bee appliqué unit on one of the remaining 11" x 14" honeycomb rectangles, positioning the bee 5" from the left and bottom edges. Fuse in place. This will be the back of the tea cozy.

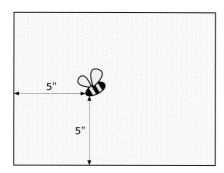

3. Machine stitch around the edges of each appliqué shape, using either a buttonhole stitch, satin stitch, or zigzag stitch.

4. Place an 11" x 14" muslin rectangle on a flat surface. Layer a batting rectangle on top of the muslin rectangle. Place one of the appliquéd rectangles on the batting rectangle, right side up; pin or spray-baste the layers together. Quilt as desired. Repeat with the remaining muslin, batting, and appliquéd rectangle.

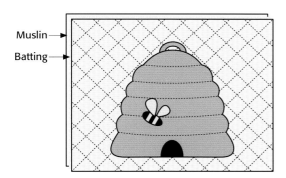

Muslin

Batting

5. To make the template for the tea cozy, photocopy or trace the pattern on page 61 onto a sheet of paper. Cut out the pattern on the outside solid line. Flip the pattern over and trace the reversed shape onto another sheet of paper; cut out the pattern on the drawn line. With the center lines butted, tape the two patterns together as shown to make the complete pattern.

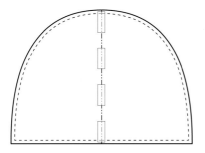

6. Place the tea cozy template on top of the quilted tea cozy front, having the bee skep centered and the bottom dashed line of the template ¼" below the appliqué stitching. Pin in place. Cut out the tea cozy front along the outer solid line. Repeat the procedure with the tea cozy back, centering the tea cozy template. Using the same template, cut 2 tea cozy shapes for the lining from the remaining two 11" x 14" honeycomb rectangles.

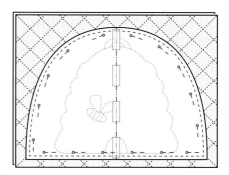

7. To make the tab for the wooden ring, press each long side of the 1" x 4" rectangle wrong sides together so that they meet in the center. Fold the strip in half lengthwise; press. Stitch close to both long edges.

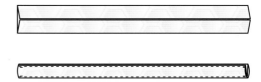

If you have difficulty with the strip not feeding under the presser foot, simply place a piece of tear-away stabilizer underneath the strip. Remove when done.

8. With right sides together, stitch the tea cozy front and back together along the curved edge, leaving ½" open in the center. Backstitch at the beginning and end of the stitching lines.

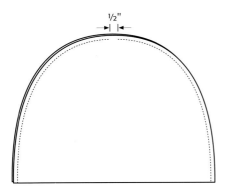

9. Remove the metal eye in the side of the wooden curtain ring by turning it counterclockwise. Fold the tab in half crosswise around the wooden ring and insert the raw edges of the tab through the ½" opening. Using a zipper foot, stitch the opening closed, stitching as close to the ring as possible, and backstitching at the beginning and end of the stitching line. Turn the tea cozy right side out.

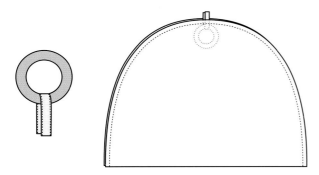

10. Using black quilting thread and the photos on pages 57 and 58 as a guide, machine stitch or hand quilt the lines from the skep entrance on the front to the bee on the back as shown.

11. Place the tea cozy lining pieces right sides together. Stitch along the curved edge, leaving a 4" opening in the center, backstitching at the beginning and end of both stitching lines. *Do not turn the lining right side out.*

12. With right sides together, place the tea cozy inside the lining, and pin the bottom raw edges together. Stitch around the entire bottom edge, overlapping the stitching line 1" at the beginning and end. Carefully pull the tea cozy through the 4" opening in the lining. Slipstitch the opening closed.

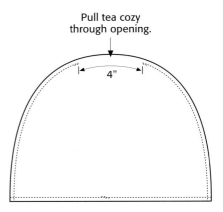

13. Insert the lining inside the tea cozy and press the edges so that they will lie flat. Topstitch ¼" from the bottom edge of the tea cozy. Using a needle and thread, hand tack the lining to the tea cozy top on the inside, stitching through all of the layers near the tab, to secure it.

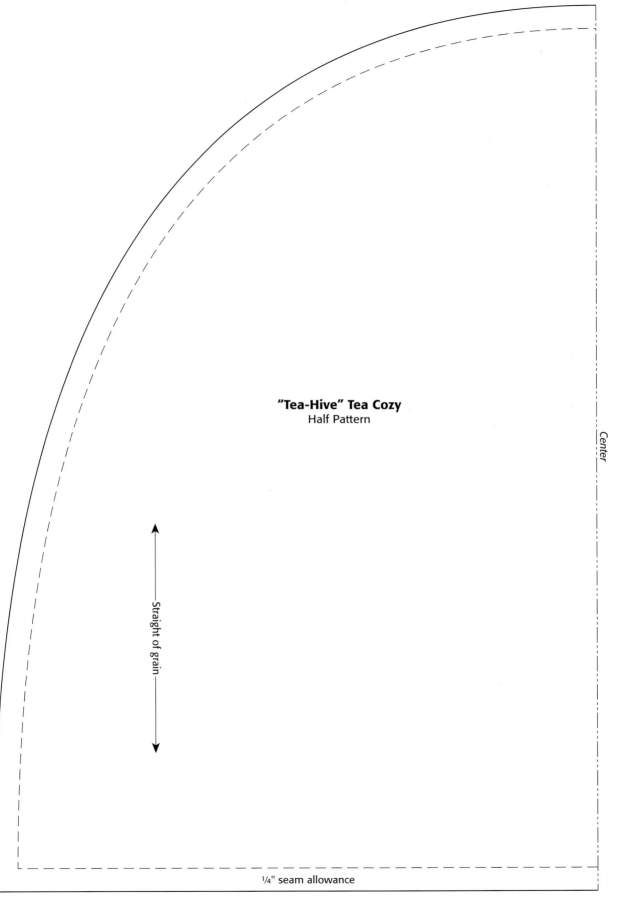

"Tea-Hive" Tea Cozy
Half Pattern

Center

Straight of grain

¼" seam allowance

"Busy Bee" Mug Rugs

A s fun as they are functional, these fabric coasters will put a smile on your face while they protect your table.

Finished mug-rug size: 4" x 4"

MATERIALS

Yardage is based on 42"-wide fabric.
Materials listed are enough to make 4 mug rugs.

- ⅜ yard of gold basket-weave print for borders and backing
- 4 squares, 4" x 4", of honeycomb print for background
- 6" x 6" square of light gray for bee wings
- 4" x 6" rectangle of black for bee bodies
- 2 strips, ¾" x 6", of yellow for bee stripes
- 4 squares, 4½" x 4½", of batting
- 6" x 8" rectangle of paper-backed fusible web
- Appliqué pressing sheet
- Black quilting thread for detail stitching
- Hand quilting needle (optional)

CUTTING

All measurements include ¼"-wide seam allowances.

From the black rectangle, cut:

1 strip, ¾" x 6", for bee bodies

2 strips, 1" x 6", for bee bodies

From the gold basket-weave print, cut:

1 strip, 4½" x 42". Crosscut to make:

- 4 squares, 4½" x 4½", for backing

2 strips, 1" x 42". Crosscut to make:

- 8 strips, 1" x 3½", for borders
- 8 strips, 1" x 4½", for borders

ASSEMBLING THE MUG-RUG TOPS

1. Referring to "Fusible-Web Appliqué" on pages 7–10, trace the bee appliqué patterns for Bee 1 on page 45 onto the paper side of the fusible web. Trace 4 *each* of D–F. *Be sure to trace the detail lines on all of the E shapes.* Cut around the shapes. Fuse shapes D and F to the wrong side of the appropriate fabrics. Cut out the appliqués on the drawn lines and remove the paper backing.

2. Referring to steps 3–5 of "Block 10: Bee Skep and Bees" on page 44, make 4 Bee 1 appliqué units.

3. Center a bee appliqué unit on the right side of each background square as shown. Fuse in place.

4. Machine stitch around the edges of each appliqué shape, using either a buttonhole stitch, satin stitch, or zigzag stitch.

Because the seam allowances in the bee bodies will prevent the appliqué unit from fusing tightly to the background fabric, you may find it helpful to use a stiletto to hold the edge down in front of the sewing-machine needle while stitching.

5. Trim the squares to 3½" x 3½", trimming evenly from each side.

6. Sew a 1" x 3½" basket-weave strip to opposite sides of each square. Press the seams toward the borders. Sew a 1" x 4½" basket-weave strip to the top and bottom edges of each square. Press the seams toward the borders.

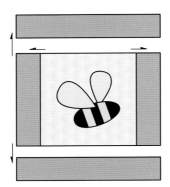

FINISHING THE MUG RUGS

1. To make each mug rug, place a batting square on a flat surface. Place a backing square on top of the batting square, right side up. Align the backing and batting edges and smooth out any wrinkles. Place an appliquéd square wrong side up over the backing. Carefully pin all of the layers together.

2. Using a walking foot, stitch the layers together along all of the edges, leaving a 2" opening along one side for turning, and backstitching at the beginning and end of the stitching line.

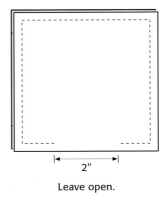

Leave open.

3. Trim the corner seam allowances to reduce bulk. Turn the mug rug right side out through the opening. Gently push the edges and corners out with a point turner. Lightly press the edges of the mug rug so that it lies flat. Slipstitch the opening closed.

4. Quilt in the ditch around the borders and around the appliqué shape. Using black quilting thread and the photo on page 62 as a guide, machine stitch or hand quilt the lines around the bee through all layers as shown.

The pairing of two techniques—appliqué and paper piecing—creates this elegant duet of banners.

Finished banner size: 7" x 19"

MATERIALS

Yardage is based on 42"-wide fabric.
Materials listed are enough to make both banners.

- ½ yard of neutral print for background
- ½ yard of floral print for appliqué letters and binding
- 6" x 7" rectangle of light rust for flowerpot
- 6" x 7" rectangle of light purple for upper flower
- 4" x 4" square of dark purple for lower flower
- 3" x 6" rectangle of yellow-orange for butterflies
- 2" x 8" rectangle of medium rust for flowerpot rim
- Scrap of medium green for stem and leaves
- Scrap of yellow for iris "beard"
- ¾ yard of fabric for backing
- 2 rectangles, 10½" x 25", of batting
- 7" x 13" rectangle of paper-backed fusible web
- Foundation paper
- Appliqué pressing sheet
- Black thread for antenna detail lines
- Hand embroidery needle (optional)
- 6" Bias Square® ruler

CUTTING

All measurements include ¼"-wide seam allowances.

From the neutral print background fabric, cut:

1 rectangle, 7" x 22", for "Spring" banner background

1 square, 6½" x 6½", for "Bearded Iris" banner background

1 square, 5⅛" x 5⅛". Cut the square in half diagonally to make 2 half-square triangles. You will use 1 triangle for the "Bearded Iris" banner point. Discard or set aside the remaining triangle.

From the floral print, cut:

4 strips, 2½" x 42", for binding

From the backing fabric, cut:

2 rectangles, 10½" x 25"

ASSEMBLING THE "SPRING" BANNER TOP

1. Referring to steps 1 and 2 of "Block 1: Spring" on page 18, make and fuse the letters to the 7" x 22" neutral rectangle, centering and positioning the shapes as shown. Machine stitch around the edge of each shape, using a satin stitch.

2. Referring to "Fusible-Web Appliqué" on pages 7–10, trace the appliqué pattern below right onto the paper side of the fusible web. Trace 2. Fuse each appliqué shape to the wrong side of the yellow-orange rectangle. Cut around the shapes. Cut out the appliqués on the drawn lines and remove the paper backing. Referring to the photo on page 65 as a guide, fuse the appliqués in place.

3. Machine stitch around the edge and detail lines of each butterfly appliqué shape, using a satin stitch and black thread. Hand or machine satin stitch the butterfly bodies using black thread. Hand embroider or machine straight stitch over the antenna detail lines using black thread.

4. Trim the rectangle to 6½" x 21½", trimming evenly from each side.

5. To create the point of the banner at the bottom edge, fold the appliquéd rectangle in half lengthwise, right sides together. Using the 6" Bias Square® ruler, place the 45° line on the ruler along the fold of the rectangle, with the corner of the ruler at the folded point of the rectangle. Trim the outer corners away from the rectangle, creating a point.

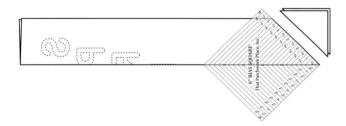

ASSEMBLING THE "BEARDED IRIS" BANNER TOP

1. Referring to "Block 7: Bearded Iris" on page 33, make 1 Bearded Iris block.

2. Sew the half-square triangle to the bottom of the flowerpot unit as shown.

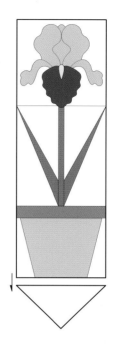

FINISHING THE BANNERS

1. Refer to "Project Finishing" on pages 13–16 to layer, quilt, and bind the banners, using the 10½" x 25" backing and batting rectangles.

2. Sew a hanging sleeve to the back of each banner.

"Spring Symphony" Banners
"Spring" Banner Appliqué Pattern

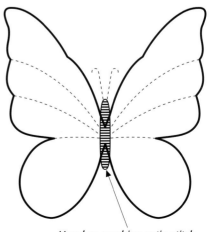

Hand or machine satin stitch butterfly body with black thread.

"Love Is in the Air" Table Runner

W ho can think of spring without thinking of bunnies? These two look like they might just fall in love! The blocks in this table runner are all appliquéd, and the border, although it may look somewhat daunting, is strip pieced for simplicity.

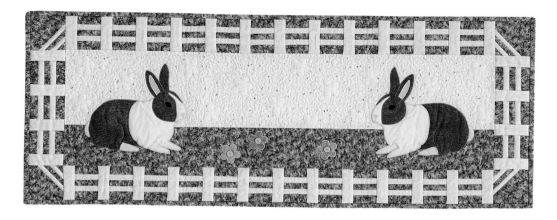

Finished table-runner size: 17" x 43"

MATERIALS

Yardage is based on 42"-wide fabric.

- ⅞ yard of green grass print for background, border, and binding
- ⅜ yard of neutral print for background
- ⅜ yard of white print for picket fence
- 7" x 14" rectangle of white for rabbit bodies, feet, and tails
- 10" x 12" rectangle of dark brown for rabbit bodies and heads
- 2" x 4" rectangle of pink for rabbit noses and inside ears
- 2½" x 2½" square of pink for flower
- 2½" x 2½" square of lavender for flower
- 2½" x 2½" square of blue for flower
- 1" x 1" square of black for rabbit eyes
- 1⅛ yards of fabric for backing
- 21" x 48" rectangle of batting
- 12" x 12" square of paper-backed fusible web
- Appliqué pressing sheet
- Heavy cardboard or template plastic
- 3 yellow ½"-diameter buttons for flower centers

CUTTING

All measurements include ¼"-wide seam allowances.

From the green grass print, cut:

1 strip, 4¼" x 42". Crosscut to make:
- 2 rectangles, 4¼" x 13", for right and left block background bottoms
- 1 rectangle, 4¼" x 14", for center block background bottom

2 strips, 1" x 42", for border blocks

4 strips, 1¼" x 42", for border blocks

1 strip, ⅞" x 21", for corner blocks

1 strip, 1¼" x 21", for corner blocks

1 strip, 3½" x 21", for corner blocks

4 strips, 2½" x 42", for binding

From the neutral print, cut:

1 strip, 7¼" x 42". Crosscut to make:
- 2 rectangles, 7¼" x 13", for right and left block background tops
- 1 rectangle, 7¼" x 14", for center block background top

From the white print, cut:

4 strips, 1" x 42", for border blocks

3 strips, 1½" x 42". Crosscut to make:
- 34 rectangles, 1½" x 3½", for border blocks

1 strip, ⅞" x 42". Crosscut to make:
- 2 strips, ⅞" x 21", for corner blocks

ASSEMBLING THE TABLE-RUNNER TOP

1. Referring to step 1 of "Block 9: Rabbit" on page 42, make the right and left background blocks using the green 4¼" x 13" and the neutral 7¼" x 13" rectangles; make the center background block using the green 4¼" x 14" and the neutral 7¼" x 14" rectangles. Using the right and left background blocks, continue with steps 2–5 of block 9, making a reverse image of one of the rabbit appliqué units.

    Note: The background rabbit blocks for the table runner are slightly larger than block 9 in the quilt, having a finished size of 10" x 12". The center block has a finished size of 10" x 13".

2. Photocopy or trace 3 flower shapes on page 72 onto the paper side of the fusible web. Cut around the shapes. Fuse each appliqué shape to the wrong side of the appropriate fabrics. Cut out the appliqués on the drawn lines and remove the paper backing. Referring to the photo on page 68, arrange the shapes on the center background block; fuse in place.

3. Machine stitch around the edges of each appliqué shape, using either a buttonhole stitch, satin stitch, or zigzag stitch.

4. Place the 3¾" line of the ruler on the seam line between the background top and bottom on the rabbit appliquéd blocks, making sure the 1" mark on the ruler is toward the bottom of the block. Trim away the excess fabric that extends beyond the ruler edge at the bottom of the block. Trim the remaining edges so that the block measures 10½" x 12½", keeping the design centered. Repeat for the remaining rabbit block. Trim the bottom edge of the center background block in the same manner. Trim the remaining edges so that the block measures 10½" x 13½".

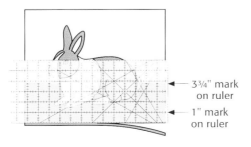

← 3¾" mark on ruler

← 1" mark on ruler

5. Sew a 1" x 42" white strip to each long side of a 1" x 42" green strip. Press the seams toward the green strip. Sew a 1¼" x 42" green strip to the long side of each white strip. Press the seams toward the green strips. Make 2. From the strip sets, cut a total of 30 segments, each 2½" wide.

    Note: If you are using a directional grass fabric, be sure to orient all of the grass strips in the same direction.

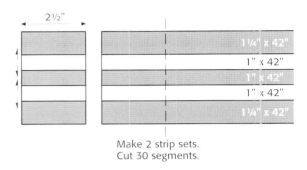

2½"

1¼" x 42"
1" x 42"
1" x 42"
1" x 42"
1¼" x 42"

Make 2 strip sets.
Cut 30 segments.

6. Sew a 1½" x 3½" white rectangle to the left side of each segment to make one border block. Press the seams toward the white rectangles.

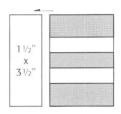

1½"
x
3½"

7. To make the top and bottom borders, sew 12 border blocks together as shown. Press the seams toward the white rectangles. Sew one of the remaining 1½" x 3½" white rectangles to the right end of the border strip. Press the seam toward the white rectangle. Make 2.

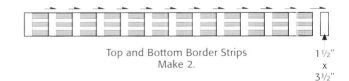

Top and Bottom Border Strips
Make 2.

1½"
x
3½"

8. To make the side borders, sew 3 border blocks together as shown. Press the seams toward the white rectangles. Sew a 1½" x 3½" white rectangle to the right end of the border strip. Press the seam toward the white rectangle. Make 2.

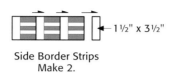

Side Border Strips
Make 2.

9. To make the corner blocks, sew a ⅞" x 21" white strip to one long side of the ⅞" x 21" green strip. Trim the seam to ⅛" and press toward the green strip. Sew the remaining ⅞" x 21" white strip to one long edge of the 1¼" x 21" green strip. Trim the seam to ⅛" and press toward the green strip. Sew these 2 strip sets together as shown. Trim the seam to ⅛" and press toward the green strip. Sew the 3½" x 21" green strip to the long, raw edge of the white strip as shown. Press the seam toward the green strip.

10. Trace the corner block pattern on page 72 onto heavy cardboard or template plastic, including the inside lines. Working on a flat cutting surface, place the template over the corner block strip set, aligning the lines on the template with the fabric strips. A portion of the green strips at the top and bottom of the strip set will extend beyond the template. Carefully cut 4 corner blocks from the strip set.

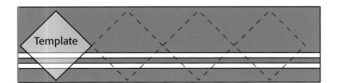

An easy and accurate way to make a template is to photocopy or trace the pattern onto plain paper. Cut out just outside the drawn lines. Using a thin coat of rubber cement, which does not cause the paper to warp as with other liquid glues, glue the paper pattern onto template plastic or cardboard. Cut out on the drawn lines.

11. Sew a corner block to opposite ends of each side border strip as shown. Press the seams toward the corner blocks. Stitch the top and bottom borders to the runner top. Press the seams away from the borders. Stitch the side borders to opposite sides of the runner top. Press the seams away from the side borders.

   Note: *If you have used directional grass fabric, verify that the grass is oriented in the correct direction before stitching.*

FINISHING THE TABLE RUNNER

1. Refer to "Project Finishing" on pages 13–16 to layer, quilt, and bind the table runner.

2. Stitch a button to the center of each flower appliqué.

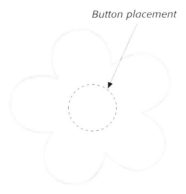

Button placement

"Love Is in the Air" Table Runner
Flower Appliqué Pattern

"Love Is in the Air" Table Runner
Corner Block Trimming Pattern

"Out on a Limb" Wall Hanging

Robins have long been considered the harbingers of spring, and this delightful couple is here to say that a new season has arrived. Why, they're already starting a family! The wall hanging is paper pieced, with a few simple appliquéd leaves on the tree.

Finished wall-hanging size: 18" x 27"

MATERIALS

Yardage is based on 42"-wide fabric.

- ½ yard of light blue for background
- ¼ yard of leaf print for border
- ⅛ yard of brown for branches
- Scrap of rust for robin breasts
- Scrap of dark gray for robin wings and heads
- Scrap of medium gray for robin backs
- Scrap of dark gold for robin beaks
- Scrap of medium blue for eggs
- Scrap of medium brown for nest
- Scrap of dark brown for inside nest
- Scrap of green for leaves
- ¾ yard of fabric for backing
- ⅜ yard of dark green for binding
- 22" x 31" rectangle of batting
- Foundation paper
- 6" x 12" rectangle of paper-backed fusible web
- Appliqué pressing sheet
- 2 black ⅛"-diameter buttons for robin eyes
- Hand embroidery needle (optional)

CUTTING

All measurements include ¼"-wide seam allowances.

From the light blue, cut:

1 rectangle, 3½" x 9½"

From the leaf print, cut:

2 strips, 3" x 42". Crosscut to make:

- 2 strips, 3" x 21½", for top and bottom borders
- 2 strips, 3" x 17½", for side borders

From the dark green, cut:

3 strips, 2½" x 42", for binding

ASSEMBLING THE WALL-HANGING TOP

1. Referring to steps 1 and 2 of "Block 11: Robin" on page 47, make 1 robin block and 1 reverse-image robin block. Do not sew a 3½" x 9½" rectangle to the left side of the blocks as indicated at the end of step 2. Instead, sew the 3½" x 9½" blue rectangle to the top of the left-facing robin block. Press the seam toward the blue rectangle.

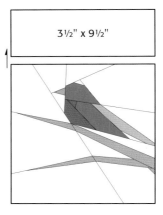

3½" x 9½"

2. Referring to "Paper Piecing" on pages 10–12, photocopy or trace the foundation patterns for the wall-hanging center unit on page 76 onto separate pieces of foundation paper. Matching the corresponding lines on section I and section II, tape the pieces of paper together to make the complete foundation pattern. Paper piece the foundation, referring to the pattern for the appropriate fabric to use in each section. Turn the pieced unit to the paper side and trim to 3½" x 12½" along the dashed lines.

3. Referring to "Paper Piecing" on pages 10–12, photocopy or trace the foundation pattern for the wall hanging bottom-right unit on page 77 onto foundation paper. Paper piece the foundation, referring to the pattern for the appropriate fabric to use in each section. Turn the pieced unit to the paper side and trim to 3½" x 9½" along the dashed lines.

4. Sew the center unit to the right edge of the left-facing robin block as shown. Press the seam toward the center unit. Sew the bottom right unit to the bottom of the right-facing robin block as shown. Press the seam toward the bottom unit. Stitch the right-facing robin block to the right edge of the center unit, carefully matching the tree intersection. Press the seam toward the center unit.

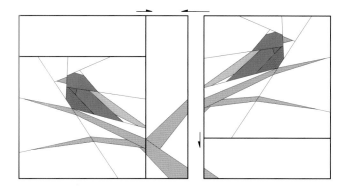

5. Referring to "Fusible-Web Appliqué" on pages 7–10, trace the appliqué patterns on page 48 onto the paper side of the fusible web. Trace 1 each of A–D and 7 of E. Cut around the shapes. Fuse each appliqué shape onto the wrong side of the appropriate fabric. Cut out the appliqués on the drawn lines and remove the paper backing. Use the nest pattern on page 48 to make a placement diagram. Using an appliqué pressing sheet and the placement diagram, fuse appliqué shapes A–D together.

6. Using the placement lines on the foundation pattern and the photo on page 73 as a guide, fuse the appliqué unit in place. Remove the paper foundation.

7. Machine stitch around the edges of each appliqué shape, using either a buttonhole stitch, satin stitch, or zigzag stitch.

8. Sew a 3" x 21½" leaf-print strip to the top and bottom edges of the wall-hanging center. Press the seams toward the borders. Sew the 3" x 17½" leaf-print strips to the sides of the wall hanging. Press the seams toward the borders.

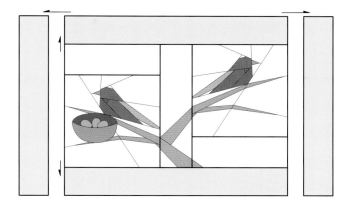

9. Referring to the photo as a guide, arrange the leaves on the wall hanging and fuse in place.

10. Machine stitch around the edges of each leaf, using either a buttonhole stitch, satin stitch, or zigzag stitch. If desired, hand or machine embroider legs and feet onto the robin on the right.

FINISHING THE WALL HANGING

1. Refer to "Project Finishing" on pages 13–16 to layer, quilt, and bind the wall hanging.

2. Sew a small black button to each bird's head where indicated for the eyes.

3. Refer to "Attaching a Hanging Sleeve" on page 16 to make and attach a sleeve for hanging.

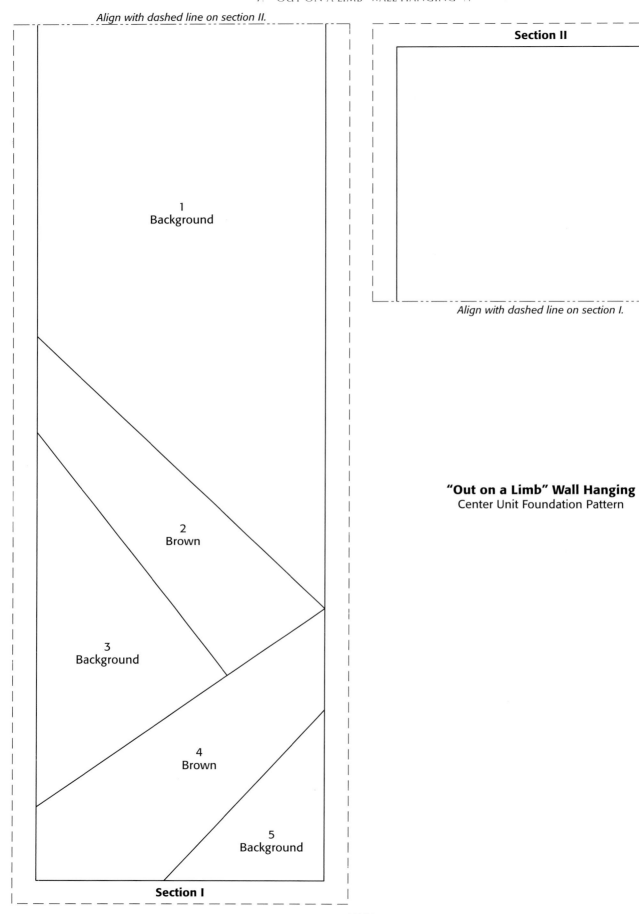

Align with dashed line on section II.

1
Background

Section II

Align with dashed line on section I.

2
Brown

3
Background

"Out on a Limb" Wall Hanging
Center Unit Foundation Pattern

4
Brown

5
Background

Section I

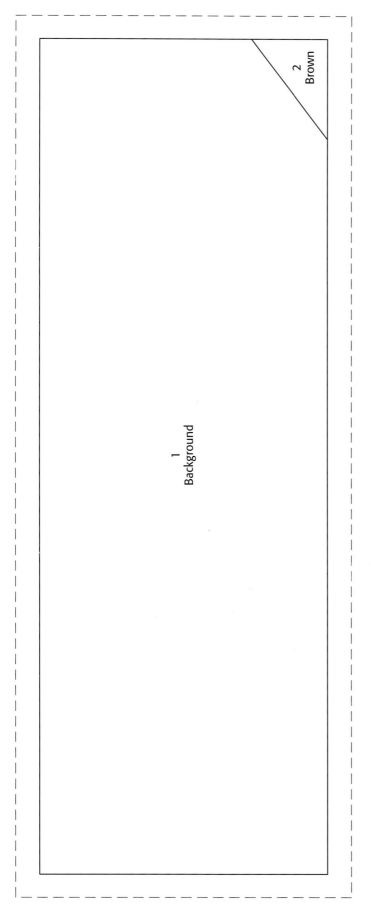

"Out on a Limb" Wall Hanging
Bottom-Right Unit
Foundation Pattern

"Spring Basket" Place Mats

These beautiful place mats would make any meal a special occasion. The baskets are paper pieced, while the flowers are appliquéd. The scalloped borders add a delicate touch, giving the mats an almost romantic feel.

Finished place-mat size: 12½" x 17½"

MATERIALS

Yardage is based on 42"-wide fabric.
Materials listed are enough to make 4 place mats.

- ¾ yard of neutral print for background
- ⅝ yard of multicolored stripe for scalloped border
- ½ yard of brown basket-weave print for basket
- ¼ yard of green for inner border and leaves
- 6" x 6" square of pink for flowers
- 6" x 6" square of blue for flowers
- 6" x 6" square of yellow #1 for flowers
- 3" x 3" square of yellow #2 for flower centers
- 1 yard of fabric for backing
- ⅞ yard of muslin
- 1 yard of low-loft batting
- Foundation paper
- 12" x 12" square of paper-backed fusible web
- Appliqué pressing sheet

CUTTING

All measurements include ¼"-wide seam allowances.

From the neutral print, cut:

2 strips, 1½" x 42". Crosscut to make:

- 8 strips, 1½" x 9½", for block sides

From the green, cut:

4 strips, 1" x 42". Crosscut to make:

- 8 strips, 1" x 14½", for top and bottom inner borders
- 8 strips, 1" x 10½", for side inner borders

From the multicolored stripe, cut:

8 strips, 2¼" x 42"

From the backing fabric, cut:

2 strips, 14" x 42". Crosscut to make:

- 8 rectangles, 14" x 10"

From the muslin, cut:

2 strips, 13" x 42". Crosscut to make:

- 4 rectangles, 13" x 18"

From the batting, cut:

4 rectangles, 13" x 18"

ASSEMBLING THE PLACE-MAT TOPS

1. Referring to "Paper Piecing" on pages 10–12, photocopy or trace 4 *each* of the foundation patterns on pages 24 and 25 onto separate pieces of foundation paper. Matching the corresponding lines on section I and section II, tape the pieces of paper together to make 4 complete foundation patterns. Paper piece the foundations, referring to the pattern for the appropriate fabric to use in each section. Turn each unit to the paper side and trim to 9½" x 12½" along the dashed lines. Carefully remove the paper foundations.

    Note: Because appliqué pieces will be added to the place mat top, the paper must be removed before the flowers are appliquéd in place. Handle the foundation pieced unit carefully so as not to distort any bias edges.

2. Referring to "Fusible-Web Appliqué" on pages 7–10, trace the appliqué patterns on page 22 onto the paper side of the fusible web. Trace 4 *each* of A–D. Also trace 4 flower centers on page 83. Cut around the shapes. Fuse each appliqué shape onto the wrong side of the appropriate fabric. Cut out the appliqués on the drawn lines and remove the paper backing. Use the patterns on page 22 to make a placement diagram. (Note that the leaf has a different placement line than on the Posies block.) Using an appliqué pressing sheet and the placement diagram, fuse the appliqué shapes together, fusing the flower center appliqué to the center of each flower last.

3. Using the placement lines on the block 3 foundation pattern and the photo on page 78 as a guide, fuse the appliqué unit in place.

4. Machine stitch around the edges of each appliqué shape, using either a buttonhole stitch, satin stitch, or zigzag stitch.

5. Sew a 1½" x 9½" background strip to opposite sides of each basket block as shown. Press the seams toward the background rectangles.

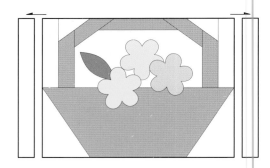

6. Sew a 1" x 14½" green inner-border strip to the top and bottom of each basket block. Press the seams toward the inner borders. Sew a 1" x 10½" green inner-border strip to the sides of each basket block. Press the seams toward the inner borders.

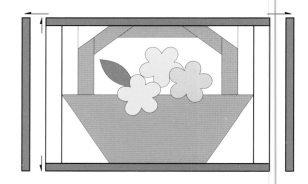

7. Referring to "Project Finishing" on pages 13–16, layer and quilt the place-mat top, using the 13" x 18" batting and muslin rectangles. Trim the batting and muslin even with the place-mat top edges.

8. To make the templates for the scalloped border, photocopy or trace the patterns on page 83 onto a sheet of paper. Cut out the patterns on the outside solid lines.

9. Place a 2¼" x 42" multicolored stripe strip on a flat surface. Fold it in half crosswise, wrong sides together, so that the ends meet. Place the top/bottom border template on one end of the strip, aligning the straight edge of the template with the cut edge of the strip and the pattern fold with the fabric fold. Pin in place. Using scissors, cut around the template. Repeat on the opposite fold of the strip. Make 8. Repeat with the side border template and the remaining 2¼" multicolored stripe strips. Make 8.

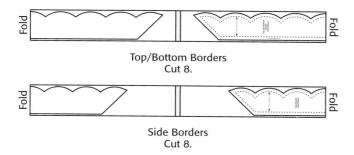

Top/Bottom Borders
Cut 8.

Side Borders
Cut 8.

10. Stitch a top/bottom border piece to the top and bottom of each place-mat center, beginning and ending ¼" from each corner and backstitching at the beginning and end of the stitching line. Press the seams toward the borders.

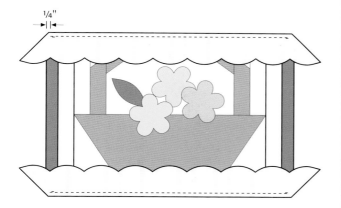

11. Stitch a side border piece to the sides of each place-mat center, beginning and ending ¼" from each corner and backstitching at the beginning and end of the stitching line. Press the seams toward the borders.

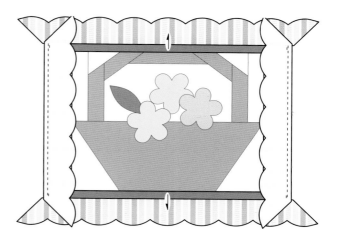

12. To stitch the mitered corners, fold a place mat diagonally, right sides together, and align the short ends of a top- and side-border strip. Beginning at the end of the previous stitching, stitch the angled ends together, ending at the scalloped edge of the border. Backstitch at the beginning of the stitching only. Repeat for all 4 sides on each place mat. Press the seams open.

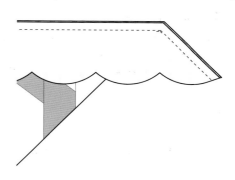

FINISHING THE PLACE MATS

1. Stitch two of the 10" x 14" backing rectangles together along the 14" edge, leaving a 5" opening in the center and backstitching at the beginning and end of the stitching lines. Press the seam open. Make 4 backing pieces.

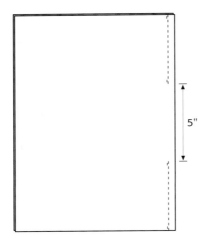

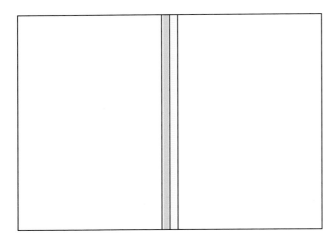

2. Place each backing rectangle on a flat surface, right side up. Lay a place-mat top on each backing rectangle, wrong side up. Pin around all edges. Stitch around all four scalloped sides. Using pinking shears, trim around the scallops close to the stitching line. Be careful not to cut

through the stitches. Cut a small notch between each scallop to reduce bulk.

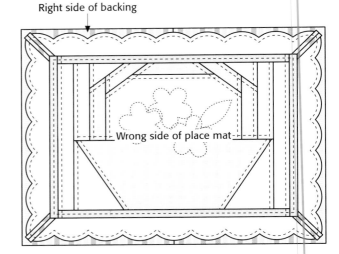

Right side of backing

Wrong side of place mat

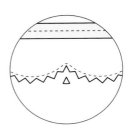

Cut out notch.

When stitching, make one straight stitch between each scallop. This will help to make a crisp turn with no puckers.

3. Turn the place mats right side out through the opening in the backing. Carefully push out the scallops of the place-mat borders, using a point turner, and making a nice smooth curve; press. Slip-stitch the openings closed. Stitch in the ditch along both sides of the inner border on each place mat to secure the backing to the front of the place mat.

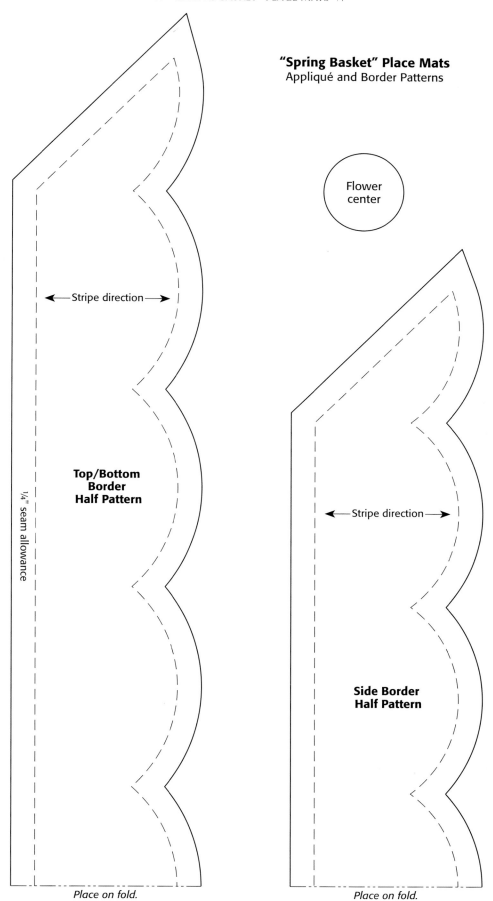

"Spring Basket" Place Mats
Appliqué and Border Patterns

Flower center

← Stripe direction →

**Top/Bottom
Border
Half Pattern**

¼" seam allowance

← Stripe direction →

**Side Border
Half Pattern**

Place on fold.

Place on fold.

"Bonnet and Bow" Pillow Sham

Not only does this pillow sham add a touch of spring to your decor, but wouldn't it also be fitting in a little girl's room? Instead of being appliquéd, the bow on the bonnet is three-dimensional and is tacked on after the pillow sham is completed. The scalloped border is the same one used for the "Spring Basket" place mats (page 78).

Finished pillow-sham size: 19½" x 19½"

MATERIALS

Yardage is based on 42"-wide fabric.

- ⅝ yard of pink for outer border and backing
- ½ yard of floral print for background
- ½ yard of multicolored stripe for scalloped border, hatband, and bow
- ¼ yard of blue for inner border
- 6" x 12" rectangle of tan weave print for bonnet
- 18" x 18" square of muslin for sham-top backing
- 18" x 18" square of batting
- 9" x 12" rectangle of paper-backed fusible web
- 6" Bias Square® ruler
- 14" to 16" throw pillow or pillow form

CUTTING

All measurements include ¼"-wide seam allowances.

From the floral print, cut:

1 square, 14½" x 14½"

From the blue, cut:

2 strips, 1" x 42". Crosscut to make:

- 2 strips, 1" x 14½", for top and bottom inner border
- 2 strips, 1" x 15½", for side inner border

From the multicolored stripe, cut:

4 strips, 2¼" x 42", for scalloped border

1 strip, 2¼" x 19", for bow streamers

1 rectangle, 4" x 3½", for bow

From the pink, cut:

2 strips, 2¾" x 42". Crosscut to make:

- 4 strips, 2¾" x 20¾", for outer borders

1 strip, 13" x 42". Crosscut to make:

- 2 rectangles, 13" x 20", for pillow-sham back

ASSEMBLING THE PILLOW-SHAM TOP

1. Referring to "Fusible-Web Appliqué" on pages 7–10, trace appliqué pattern A on page 30 and appliqué pattern B on page 88 onto the paper side of the fusible web. Cut around the shapes. Fuse each appliqué shape onto the wrong side of the appropriate fabric. Cut out the appliqués on the drawn lines and remove the paper backing. Fuse shape A onto the floral-print square as shown. Fuse shape B on top of shape A where indicated on the appliqué pattern on page 30.

   Note: Unlike the quilt block, shape B will extend all the way across the crown of the hat on the pillow sham.

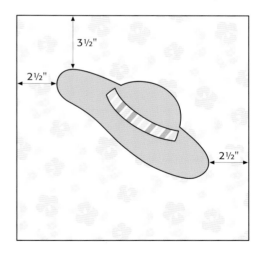

2. Machine stitch around the edges of each appliqué shape, using either a buttonhole stitch, satin stitch, or zigzag stitch.

3. Sew a 1" x 14½" blue inner-border strip to the top and bottom of the pillow-sham center. Press the seams toward the inner border. Sew a

1" x 15½" blue inner-border strip to the sides of the pillow-sham center. Press the seams toward the inner border.

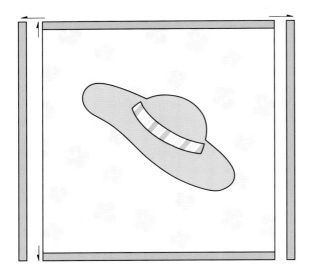

4. Referring to "Project Finishing" on pages 13–16, layer and quilt the pillow-sham top, using the 18" x 18" batting and muslin squares. Trim the batting and muslin even with the top edges of the sham.

5. To make the bow, fold the 3½" x 4" striped rectangle in half lengthwise, right sides together. Stitch the raw edges together, leaving a 1" opening at the center for turning. Backstitch at the beginning and end of the stitching lines. Trim the corners and turn the rectangle to the right side; press. Slip-stitch the opening closed.

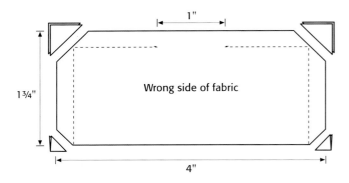

1"

1¾"

Wrong side of fabric

4"

6. To make the streamers, fold the 2¼" x 19" striped strip in half lengthwise, right sides together. Using the Bias Square® ruler, cut the ends at an angle as shown. Stitch the raw edges

together, leaving a 1½" opening in the center for turning. Backstitch at the beginning and end of the stitching lines. Trim the corners and turn the strip to the right side; press. Slip-stitch the opening closed.

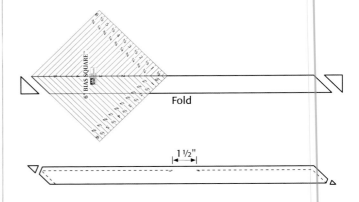

Fold

1½"

7. Fold the streamer in half crosswise, offsetting the center by 1". Stitch across the strip, ½" from the fold line. Backstitch at the beginning and end of the stitching line to reinforce the edges. Insert the bow piece from step 5 through the loop in the streamer strip. Adjust the folds of the bow if necessary. Set aside.

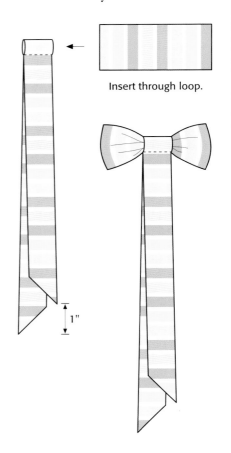

Insert through loop.

1"

8. To make the template for the scalloped border, photocopy or trace the place-mat top/bottom border pattern on page 83 onto a sheet of paper. Cut out the pattern on the outside solid line. Flip the pattern over and trace the reversed shape onto another sheet of paper; cut out the pattern on the drawn line. With the center lines butted, tape the 2 patterns together as shown to make the complete pattern.

9. Place a 2¼" x 42" striped strip on a flat surface. Fold it in half crosswise, right sides together. Place the top/bottom border template on the strip, aligning the straight edge of the template with the cut edge of the strip. Pin in place. Using scissors, cut around the template. Carefully remove the template without disturbing the fabric. Stitch the two border pieces together *along the scalloped edges only*. With pinking shears, trim the seam allowance close to the stitching line, being careful not to clip into the threads. Snip a notch between each scallop. Turn right side out and press, smoothing out the scallops with a point turner. Repeat to make 3 more border strips.

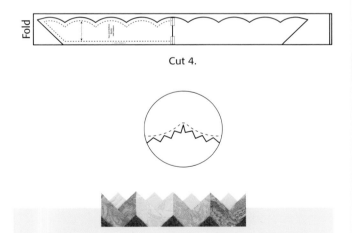

Cut 4.

When stitching, make one straight stitch between each scallop. This will help make a crisp turn with no puckers.

10. Using a Bias Square® ruler, trim the ends of each 2¾" x 20¾" pink strip to 45° as shown. Machine baste one of the scalloped borders to each of the pink strips along the straight edge, using a scant ¼" seam allowance.

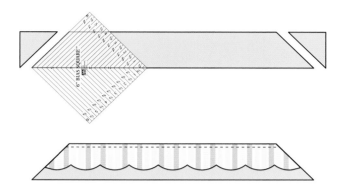

11. Stitch the pillow-sham borders to the pillow-sham top, referring to steps 10–12 of the place-mat instructions on page 81 to attach the borders and miter the corners.

FINISHING THE PILLOW SHAM

1. Press under ¼" along one long side of each of the 12⅞" x 19¾" sham-back rectangles. Press under ¼" again and stitch the edges in place.

2. Place the sham-back rectangles on a flat surface, wrong sides up. Overlap the finished ends 5", keeping the top and bottom edges of each rectangle aligned as shown. Verify that the piece measures 19¾" x 19¾". Make any necessary adjustments, and then pin the overlapped

edges together. Machine baste the raw edges together using a scant ¼" seam allowance.

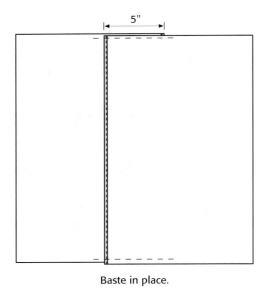

Baste in place.

3. Pin the sham top and back right sides together. Stitch around all 4 sides. Trim the corners. Turn the sham to the right side through the opening in the back. Push out the corners with a point turner. Lightly press the edges of the pillow sham.

4. From the front of the pillow sham, stitch in the ditch between the inner border and the scalloped border, stitching through all layers, to create a flange.

5. Referring to the photo on page 84, tack the bow to the bonnet band. Insert the throw pillow or pillow form into the sham.

"Bonnet and Bow" Pillow Sham
Appliqué Pattern

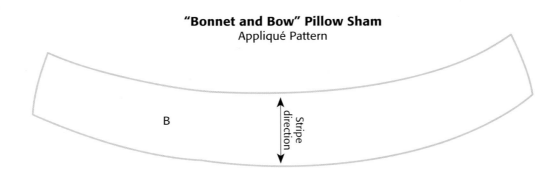

B

Stripe direction

"April Showers" Wall Hanging and "Crocus Chorus" Shelf Quilt

The two-part wall hanging is joined by satin ribbons that depict water streaming from a watering can spout. Both units are paper pieced and use the background fabric for binding, allowing the background to recede and make the watering can and tulips the focus.

In the shelf quilt, tiny 3" paper-pieced Crocus blocks are sewn together on point. What an easy way to dress up an otherwise neglected area of the house! While the pictured shelf quilt uses five blocks and measures only 30" long, you could easily customize it to fit a longer shelf by adding more blocks.

"APRIL SHOWERS" WALL HANGING

Finished watering-can-unit size: 17½" x 17½"

Finished tulip-unit size: 6½" x 18½"

MATERIALS

Yardage is based on 42"-wide fabric.

- ¾ yard of neutral print for background and binding
- ⅓ yard or 1 fat quarter of gray for watering can
- ¼ yard of medium green for leaves
- Scraps of medium pink, medium lavender, and medium yellow for flower petals
- Scraps of dark pink, dark lavender, and dark yellow for flower centers
- Foundation paper
- 3 yards of ⅛"-wide light blue double-faced satin ribbon for "water"
- Silk ribbon embroidery needle

CUTTING

All measurements include ¼"-wide seam allowances.

From the neutral print, cut:

2 squares, 9⅜" x 9⅜"; cut each square in half diagonally to make 4 half-square triangles for watering-can-unit setting triangles

4 strips, 2½" x 42", for binding

ASSEMBLING THE WALL-HANGING TOPS

1. Referring to "Block 8: Watering Can" on page 38, make 1 Watering Can block.

2. Stitch the long side of 2 setting triangles to the top and bottom of the Watering Can block. Press the seams toward the setting triangles. Stitch the long side of the 2 remaining setting triangles to the sides of the Watering Can block. Press the seams toward the setting triangles.

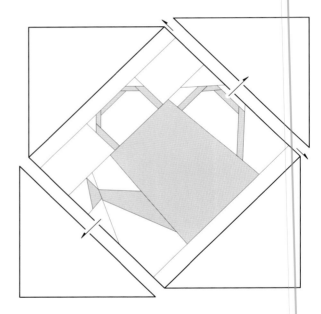

3. Referring to "Block 4: Tulip" on page 26, make 3 Tulip blocks. Sew the blocks together into a horizontal strip as shown. Press the seams open.

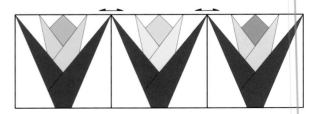

FINISHING THE WALL HANGINGS

1. Refer to "Project Finishing" on pages 13–16 to layer, quilt, and bind the 2 wall hangings.

2. Refer to "Attaching a Hanging Sleeve" on page 16 to make and attach a hanging sleeve to each of the wall hangings.

3. After the wall hangings are completed, connect them using the blue satin ribbon. Place the watering-can wall hanging on a flat surface. Place the tulip wall hanging 3" below, having the seam between the second and third tulips directly under the left edge of the watering-can wall hanging.

4. Cut the ribbon into 5 lengths, 20" long. Thread the needle with a length of satin ribbon and make a knot in one end. Insert the needle from the back of the watering can spout through X #1 and pull the ribbon through to the front until the knot makes contact with the back. Twist the ribbon several times. Then insert it through the tip of the far-left tulip as shown. Make a knot in the ribbon at the back of the tulip to secure the ribbon in place. Repeat this step 4 more times until all of the ribbons are in place, inserting ribbons 1, 3, and 5 through the tips of the tulips and ribbons 2 and 4 between each Tulip block.

Note: When arranging this wall hanging on the wall, remember to arrange the tulips as shown.

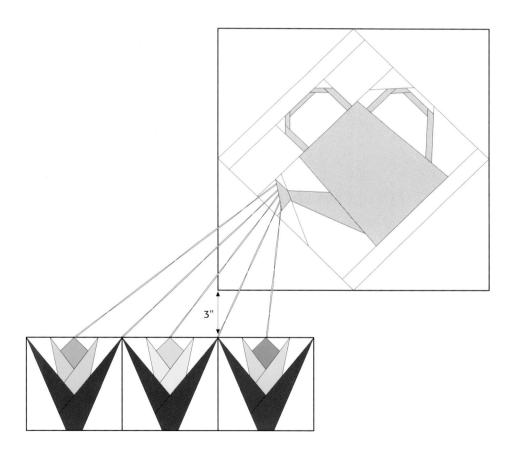

3"

"CROCUS CHORUS" SHELF QUILT

Finished shelf-quilt size: 6" x 30"

MATERIALS

Yardage is based on 42"-wide fabric.

- ¾ yard of neutral print for background and shelf piece
- ½ yard of fabric for backing*
- Scrap of medium green for leaves
- Scraps of light pink, blue, lavender, and yellow marble for flower petals
- Scrap of solid yellow for flower centers
- 16" x 34" rectangle of lightweight batting or flannel*
- Foundation paper

* This amount is enough for shelves with a depth of up to 8". For deeper shelves, adjust the yardage accordingly.

CUTTING

All measurements include ¼"-wide seam allowances.

From the neutral print, cut:

1 strip, 3" x 42". Crosscut to make:

- 10 squares, 3" x 3"; cut each square in half diagonally to make 20 half-square triangles for block corners

1 square, 7¼" x 7¼"; cut in half diagonally twice to make 4 quarter-square triangles for shelf-quilt setting triangles

1 square, 3⅞" x 3⅞"; cut in half diagonally to make 2 half-square triangles for shelf-quilt corners

1 strip, shelf depth x 30½", for shelf piece*

From the backing fabric, cut:

1 strip, 6½" + shelf depth x 30½"*

From the batting, cut:

1 strip, 6½" + shelf depth x 30½"*

> ** Measure the depth of the shelf (from the back wall to the front edge of the shelf) on which the shelf quilt will hang. Add ½" to this measurement.*

ASSEMBLING THE SHELF-QUILT TOP

1. Referring to "Paper Piecing" on pages 10–12, use the pattern on page 51 to photocopy or trace 5 Crocus foundations onto foundation paper. Paper piece the foundations, referring to the pattern for the appropriate fabric to use in each section. Turn the blocks to the paper side and trim to 3½" x 3½" along the dotted lines. Remove the paper.

2. Stitch the long side of 2 triangles (cut from the 3" squares) to the top and bottom of each Crocus block. Press the seams toward the triangles. Stitch the long side of the remaining corner triangles to the sides of each Crocus block. Press the seams toward the corner triangles.

3. Stitch the short side of a quarter-square setting triangle to the top left side of 4 Crocus blocks. Press the seams toward the setting triangles.

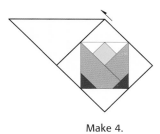

Make 4.

4. Stitch the long side of a half-square corner triangle to the upper-left side of the remaining Crocus block and the upper-right side of one of the blocks from step 3.

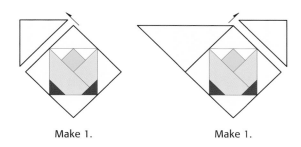

Make 1.　　　　Make 1.

5. Stitch the Crocus blocks together as shown. Press the seams in the directions indicated. Twisting the seam allowance to press adjoining triangles in opposite directions may seem awkward, but it makes sewing the backing to the quilt top easier.

   Note: *The edges of the Crocus blocks will extend ¼" beyond the seam line of the setting triangles.*

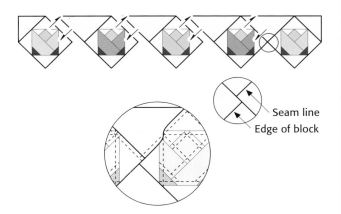

Seam line
Edge of block

6. Stitch the long edge of the shelf piece to the straight edge of the crocus unit. Press the seam toward the shelf piece.

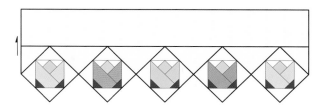

FINISHING THE SHELF QUILT

1. Place the batting or flannel on a flat surface. Layer the backing right side up on top of the batting. Then layer the shelf-quilt top, wrong side up. Smooth out any wrinkles and pin around all 4 sides through all layers. Using a walking foot, stitch around all 4 sides, leaving a 6" opening along the straight edge for turning. Trim ¼" from the Crocus block raw edges. Trim the corners and points and turn the shelf quilt right side out through the opening. Gently push out the corners and points with a point turner. Slip-stitch the opening closed.

Batting　Backing　　6"

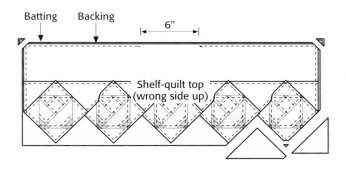

Shelf-quilt top
(wrong side up)

2. Stitch along the shelf-piece seam line through all layers to secure. Fold along the same seam line and press to form a crease where the unit will hang over the shelf.

Stitch in the ditch

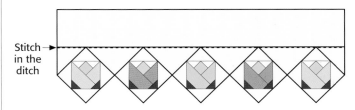

Resources

Peace By Piece Designs®
PO Box 350
Ashton, IL 61006
(815) 453-2055
Toll-free (866) 447-8458
www.PeaceByPieceDesigns.com
Appliqué pressing sheet, Clover white marking pen

Ackfeld Manufacturing
PO Box 539
Reeds Spring, MO 65737
www.ackfeldwire.com and also available
through www.PeaceByPieceDesigns.com
Classic Motifs 7½" craft holder (shown on page 65)

Elizabeth's Creative Quilting
7407 F.M. 3180
Baytown, TX 77520
(281) 573-1430
www.elizabethsquiltshop.com
Custom machine quilting

Marble-T Designs
(520) 731-0895
www.marbledfab.com
Hand-marbled fine art fabrics

Starr Designs, Inc.
P.O. Box 440
Etna, CA 96027
(530) 467-5121
www.starrfabrics.com
Hand-dyed fabrics

About the Author

Lois Krushina Fletcher is a self-taught quilter who began quilting in 1990. Quilting quickly replaced her numerous other hobbies, becoming her passion and, eventually, her career. In 2000 she began her own pattern design company, Peace By Piece Designs®. Since then she has published numerous patterns as well as the first two books in her Quilter's Home series, *The Quilter's Home: Fall* and *The Quilter's Home: Winter*. Inspired by the success of this series, Lois is debuting a new line of patterns called Patterns with a Purpose™, which will focus on simple, coordinated home-decor items.

Lois has appeared on the television program *Quilting with Shar,* and her work has been published in *Quilts and Coordinates*, a magazine that focuses on decorating with quilted items. She has also designed a variety of Quilt-a-Cards note cards for Paper Creations.

Lois spent most of her life in the South, but an unexpected move in 2002 brought her to the village of Ashton in northern Illinois. She resides there with her husband, four very special cats, and a Samoyed named Misty. She has two grown sons, Michael and Matthew (and a beautiful daughter-in-law, Jennifer), who reside in Texas. Lois is enjoying her new life in the Midwest. She and her husband are renovating an old house (circa 1916), which has a spectacular attic destined to become her studio.

Though time doesn't currently allow for many hobbies, one of her longstanding favorites is gardening. When she isn't working in the kitchen trying to keep up with her garden's bounty, she spends her time creating new designs for her ever-growing pattern line. You can see more of her patterns by visiting her Web site at www.PeaceByPieceDesigns.com.

New and Bestselling Titles from

America's Best-Loved Craft & Hobby Books®
America's Best-Loved Knitting Books®

America's Best-Loved Quilt Books®

NEW RELEASES
300 Paper-Pieced Quilt Blocks
American Doll Quilts
Classic Crocheted Vests
Dazzling Knits
Follow-the-Line Quilting Designs
Growing Up with Quilts
Hooked on Triangles
Knitting with Hand-Dyed Yarns
Lavish Lace
Layer by Layer
Lickety-Split Quilts
Magic of Quiltmaking, The
More Nickel Quilts
More Reversible Quilts
No-Sweat Flannel Quilts
One-of-a-Kind Quilt Labels
Patchwork Showcase
Pieced to Fit
Pillow Party!
Pursenalities
Quilter's Bounty
Quilting with My Sister
Seasonal Quilts Using Quick Bias
Two-Block Appliqué Quilts
Ultimate Knitted Tee, The
Vintage Workshop, The
WOW! Wool-on-Wool Folk Art Quilts

APPLIQUÉ
Appliquilt in the Cabin
Blossoms in Winter
Garden Party
Shadow Appliqué
Stitch and Split Appliqué
Sunbonnet Sue All through the Year

Our books are available at
bookstores and your favorite
craft, fabric, and yarn retailers.
If you don't see the title
you're looking for, visit us at
www.martingale-pub.com
or contact us at:

1-800-426-3126

International: 1-425-483-3313
Fax: 1-425-486-7596
Email: info@martingale-pub.com

6/04

HOLIDAY QUILTS & CRAFTS
Christmas Cats and Dogs
Christmas Delights
Hocus Pocus!
Make Room for Christmas Quilts
Welcome to the North Pole

LEARNING TO QUILT
101 Fabulous Rotary-Cut Quilts
Happy Endings, Revised Edition
Loving Stitches, Revised Edition
More Fat Quarter Quilts
Quilter's Quick Reference Guide, The
Sensational Settings, Revised Edition
Simple Joys of Quilting, The
Your First Quilt Book (or it should be!)

PAPER PIECING
40 Bright and Bold Paper-Pieced Blocks
50 Fabulous Paper-Pieced Stars
Down in the Valley
Easy Machine Paper Piecing
For the Birds
Papers for Foundation Piecing
Quilter's Ark, A
Show Me How to Paper Piece
Traditional Quilts to Paper Piece

QUILTS FOR BABIES & CHILDREN
Easy Paper-Pieced Baby Quilts
Easy Paper-Pieced Miniatures
Even More Quilts for Baby
More Quilts for Baby
Quilts for Baby
Sweet and Simple Baby Quilts

ROTARY CUTTING/SPEED PIECING
365 Quilt Blocks a Year Perpetual
  Calendar
1000 Great Quilt Blocks
Burgoyne Surrounded
Clever Quarters
Clever Quilts Encore
Endless Stars
Once More around the Block
Pairing Up
Stack a New Deck
Star-Studded Quilts
Strips and Strings
Triangle-Free Quilts

SCRAP QUILTS
Easy Stash Quilts
Nickel Quilts
Rich Traditions
Scrap Frenzy
Successful Scrap Quilts

TOPICS IN QUILTMAKING
Asian Elegance
Batiks and Beyond
Bed and Breakfast Quilts
Coffee-Time Quilts
Dutch Treat
English Cottage Quilts
Fast-Forward Your Quilting
Machine-Embroidered Quilts
Mad about Plaid!
Romantic Quilts
Simple Blessings

CRAFTS
20 Decorated Baskets
Beaded Elegance
Blissful Bath, The
Collage Cards
Creating with Paint
Holidays at Home
Pretty and Posh
Purely Primitive
Stamp in Color
Trashformations
Warm Up to Wool
Year of Cats…in Hats!, A

KNITTING & CROCHET
365 Knitting Stitches a Year Perpetual
  Calendar
Beyond Wool
Classic Knitted Vests
Crocheted Aran Sweaters
Crocheted Lace
Crocheted Socks!
Garden Stroll, A
Knit it Now!
Knits for Children and Their Teddies
Knits from the Heart
Knitted Throws and More
Knitter's Template, A
Little Box of Scarves, The
Little Box of Sweaters, The
Style at Large
Today's Crochet
Too Cute! Cotton Knits for Toddlers